Border Crossings and Beyond

WOMEN WRITERS OF COLOR

Border Crossings and Beyond

The Life and Works of Sandra Cisneros

Carmen Haydée Rivera

Joanne M. Braxton, Series Editor

PRAEGER

An Imprint of ABC-CLIO, LLC

A B C ⬤ C L I O

Santa Barbara, California • Denver, Colorado • Oxford, England

Library of Congress Cataloging-in-Publication Data
Rivera, Carmen Haydée.
    Border crossings and beyond : the life and works of Sandra Cisneros / Carmen Haydée Rivera.
        p. cm. — (Women writers of color)
    Includes bibliographical references and index.
    ISBN 978-0-313-34518-0 (alk. paper) — ISBN 978-0-313-34519-7 (ebook)
    1. Cisneros, Sandra. I. Title.
    PS3553.I78Z85 2010
    813'.54—dc22
    [B]
                                        2009032315
13 12 11 10 9 1 2 3 4 5

This book is also available on the World Wide Web as an eBook.
Visit www.abc-clio.com for details.

ABC-CLIO, LLC
130 Cremona Drive, P.O. Box 1911
Santa Barbara, California 93116-1911

This book is printed on acid-free paper ∞
Manufactured in the United States of America

For Diana,
hermana, amiga, confidente,
for the strength of the ties
that bind us
throughout our border crossings

And for my goddaughters,
Jasmin and Camille,
the next generation of
border crossers

con el cariño de siempre…

Contents

Series Foreword

The Women Writers of Color biography series was created to celebrate the lives and letters of women writers of African American, Asian American, Native American, and U.S. Latina descent; it is designed to inform and to delight a multicultural audience that knows both the cost and the necessity of creativity. This series exists for every woman writer of color whose work we will never know; it exists for everyone of every race who can read or hear these words and appreciate them; it exists for every little girl of any race whoever wrote a poem and hid it; and it exists for daughters of those mothers whose creativity and intelligence were suppressed, hidden, targeted, or denied. It opens the way for literary works that have been overlooked for too long to find their well-deserved places in our libraries and on our bookshelves. Each biographical volume is published with a user friendly bibliography so that readers can pursue original readings by these authors and find existing literary criticism more readily.

We are proud to present *Border Crossings and Beyond: The Life and Works of Sandra Cisneros* by Carmen Haydée Rivera, the first biography in the Women Writers of Color series to explore the formidable body of literature blooming as a defiant testament of creativity and transcendence among Latina writers living and working at the borderlands of geography and consciousness. Sandra Cisneros, born in Chicago of a Mexican father and a Mexican American mother, represents the Tex-Mex border as a "site of memory" that extends into the heart of North America. *La Frontera* simultaneously unites and divides generations of Mexicans and Mexican Americans who share ancient bloodlines, rich linguistic traditions, and sacred mythology, including the remembrance of an ancestral homeland, sometimes referred to as Aztlán. Cisneros' work, like that of many of her sisters, grapples with a profound sense of dislocation and displacement with subtlety, dignity, grace, and sass; her words rise like a magical incantation, a prayer or invocation for wholeness and liberation in the face of everything that tears, divides, and disrupts.

Through her body of work embracing fiction, poetry, and essay, Sandra Cisneros symbolically becomes *La Llorona*, the weeping woman, a Tex-Mex avenger, signifying both tradition and continuity with her ancestral past. And yet, her cries transcend the particular heritage and social location from which she speaks to embrace the universal with deftly nuanced sophistication, wonder, and awe: "So many *milagritos* safety-pinned here, so many little miracles dangling from a red thread-a gold Sacred Heart, a tiny copper arm, a kneeling man in silver, a bottle, a brass truck, a foot, a house, a hand, a baby, a cat, a breast, a tooth, a belly button, an evil eye. So many petitions, so many promises made and kept." (From the short story "Little Miracles, Kept Promises" in *Woman Hollering Creek and Other Stories* (New York: Vintage, 1991), 116–129.) A maker and keeper of promises, Cisneros presents a post-colonial jeremiad that is at once lamentation and celebration. This is work that afflicts the comfortable and comforts the afflicted, strengthening the weary for struggle in an often oppressive environment of blue-eyed Barbie doll "normalcy," where Yanqui imperialism, sexism, heterosexism, racism, and classism are most often still firmly entrenched. Together with her literary sistren, Cisneros is *comadre*, *maccomere*, or *comother*, birthing a r/evolution of the human spirit in a never ending, always extending spiral of recognition and self-conscious growth. She challenges the politics of domination at every turn, no matter whether it presents itself as racial, class, or sexual oppression. With words and images, she creates a psychic geography or sanctuary some might even call holy ground, ground a next generation of women of color writers can claim as home. It need only be re-visited, not re-invented. This is art, yes; it is also education for liberation.

There could be no better interpreter of this life and this body of literature than Carmen Haydée Rivera, Associate Professor of English at the University of Puerto Rico, Rio Piedras. Born in Puerto Rico and raised in Boston in a family determined to maintain a connection with its Puerto Rican roots, Professor Rivera has navigated a different *frontera*, but one that resonates with the larger terrain wherein she is making her mark as a scholar and critic. With José L. Torres-Padilla, Rivera co-edited *Writing Off the Hyphen: New Perspectives on the Literature of the Puerto-Rican Diaspora* (2008). Widely published in journals, this is her debut single-author volume, a rich treatment of the remarkable life and career of Sandra Cisneros that is yet and still unfolding. In this literary biography, Professor Rivera, from her own unique perspective, examines the relationships between Cisneros' life as lived and the ways in which the artist represents those she gathers as her people, interrogating and crossing boundaries of genre, gender, race, class, and consciousness. Rivera illuminates historical and cultural contexts crucial to the overall understanding of Cisneros' works, focusing on the ways Cisneros assumes the task of bearing witness to the constantly evolving immigrant experience of a multiethnic/multicultural

America by inserting her own mixed and/or blended languages, cultures, and worldviews into the U.S. literary scene. Let us then welcome *Border Crossings and Beyond: The Life and Works of Sandra Cisneros* and Carmen Haydée Rivera to the community of women of color writers and scholars who advance what our foremothers began, forging a space for creation and analysis of literary works that honor our richly diverse lives.

Gracias a Dios. So may it be. Amen. Amin. Ashé.
Joanne M. Braxton
College of William and Mary
Series Editor

Acknowledgments

Working on this project and scrutinizing Sandra Cisneros' life and works so intensely has provided a world of new experiences and challenges that I had not anticipated when I accepted the assignment. Having read, analyzed, and taught Cisneros' works for so long in my classes on Latino(a) literature initially convinced me that this was an endeavor I had to be involved in and one that I knew would strengthen and nourish not only my academic experience but also my affiliation with the many women whose works have shaped a whole generation of Latina scholars and many more to come.

So first and foremost, I wish to thank Sandra Cisneros for her inspiring life story, but most of all for her creativity, tenacity, and spirit, for her unwavering support of all causes Latino(a), and for always striving to move past demarcations of class, race, and gender to a world beyond borders. The quintessential image of her inner strength is readily captured by Puerto Rican artist settled in San Antonio, Angel Rodríguez-Díaz, whose beautiful portrait adorns this book cover. *Gracias, Angel, por tu generosidad y talento artístico y porque el destino nos unió en esta colaboración.*

Deepest gratitude goes to my colleague and friend María Soledad Rodríguez for bringing this project to my attention and for her generosity and support that dates back to the time we met more than two decades ago.

To the series editor, Dr. Joanne Braxton, for her interest in the continued analysis and dissemination of literary works by women of color writers, and for her patience throughout the publication process, I thank you dearly. I also commend Greenwood Press/ABC-CLIO for spearheading such a worthy project and for their commitment to women's literature.

Special thanks go to my research assistants, Miguel Meléndez and Naida García, for locating and cataloguing valuable bibliographic sources and materials on Cisneros, which facilitated preparation for the writing process. And to my friend Norma Cantú, for helping me with specific Chicano(a) terminology that sometimes eluded my comprehension. I also admire her inspiring poise and composure at all times, which motivated me to keep focused.

Last but not least, my deepest appreciation for Axel's continued support and encouragement, for being the feminist husband I imagined as a life partner and was especially blessed with in more ways than one. *Gracias, gracias, gracias, y todo mi amor por siempre.*

In celebrating Cisneros' life and works, I also pay tribute to her extended family as well as to her Mexican roots and heritage. In this same vein, I also honor my own family, *en especial a mis padres, hermana y hermanos,* whose stories of migration from and/or relocation back to Puerto Rico have shaped my own appreciation of the bilingual, bicultural world we inhabit.

Naming, Narrating, Knowing: The Chicana Experience and the Literary Text

Ideally, each of our serious conversations with one another is like a "new world." What we bring is questions, ultimately, not answers. We search together, bringing our best selves to the task. . . .

—Pat Mora

During the United Nations' Fourth World Women's Conference celebrated in Beijing, China, (1995), Irene Isabel Blea spoke about the status of Chicanas and other Latinas in the United States. Her observations and concerns were later collected in *U.S. Chicanas and Latinas Within a Global Context*.[1] Blea's arguments provide important intersections of race, culture, and gender that lead to a reevaluation of the ways in which Chicana and other Latina authors have approached the act of writing. In her discussion, Blea describes *la Chicana* as:

a Mexican-American female who has minority status in her own land even though she is, in part, indigenous to the Americas and a member of one of the largest (minority) ethnic groups in the United States. She is a woman whose life is too often characterized by poverty, racism, and sexism not only in the dominant culture but also within her own culture. Chicanas are also not characterized

as members of a conquering and conquered culture rooted in the Spanish language. . . . These women are . . . often lumped together with other U.S. Latinas
(Puerto Rican, Cuban, Central and South American) as if there were no diversity
among [them]. These women are also U.S. citizens with full legal rights and
responsibilities for whom there is unofficial discrimination.[2]

Blea adds that what we witness when we see a Chicana today "took over five
hundred years in the making,"[3] a product of mixed races (Indian, Spanish,
Mexican, American), Christianity, and patriarchy. Yet what Blea insistently criticizes throughout her work is the blatant disregard for the ways in which many
Latinas have historically risen above their disenfranchised status and managed
to confront acts of discrimination and exclusion through perseverance, education, and social engineering. Blea further acknowledges that contemporary
Latinas have also been influenced by a growing sense of female consciousness;
feminism; social, racial, and political struggle; and resistance. This affirmative
position, and her attendance at the Beijing conference, lead Blea to conclude
that "U.S. Latinas are highly resilient and tenacious. Cultural and historical
social conditions have demanded that females develop strong character,"
which implies "developing a consciousness that cannot be explained by the
internal colonial method of oppression. They [Latinas] are going beyond a call
for decolonization, and they are doing it for themselves because they have
learned that their oppressor will not."[4]

Writing, then, becomes a means through which Latinas insert themselves
and their concerns into militant platforms that call for radical change and, consequently, into Latino/a and Anglo American social contexts. Sandra Cisneros,
one of the most prominent Chicana writers to date, exemplifies this militancy.
An appropriate starting point from which to inscribe Cisneros' experience
within these platforms and social contexts is to examine her life story and the
factors that contribute to her literary development.

Chicanos/as have ignited significant debates and participated in controversial events since their tumultuous historical beginnings. This designation is
rooted in the Civil Rights Movement of the 1960s, defended by *El Plan Espir-
itual de Aztlán*,[5] and spurred by the demands of students and faculty members
in major universities across the nation.[6] A call for more cultural, social, and
political representation of *La Raza* (a cultural revolution and awareness of
"Mexicanism" and Latino heritage) in the academy and in society at large was
the focus of these demands.[7] Initially, Chicanos and Chicanas were united
against a common front. They rejected capitalism, imperialism, and inequality
based on social and racial divisions. Adopting a socialist perspective, they participated in marches, organized strikes, and worked on strategies that would
improve their participation within social-political structures.[8]

Chicanas participated in every stage in the formation of a new political
Chicano/a class. Nevertheless, Chicanas' struggles were seldom given rightful
recognition. Norma Alarcón points out that failure to acknowledge women's
participation in the movement "is indicative of the process of erasure and

exclusion of raced ethnic women within a patriarchal cultural and political economy."[9] An interesting literary portrayal that parallels the ways in which Chicanas were depicted and how their struggles played out within the Chicano Movement appears in Dolores Prida's play *Beautiful Señoritas* in the characterization of the *guerrillera*.[10] This character spurs the other women in the play into action by calling for a united force to fight for equality and defend their rights. Once the women are rallied in support of their causes and ready to change the world, the *guerrillera* steps back for a second to instruct the others: "But first, hold it . . . , we must peel the potatoes, cook the rice, make the menudo and sweep the hall (*The WOMEN groan and lose enthusiasm*) because there's going to be a fundraiser tonight!"[11] The play indicts the fact that women were assigned menial roles within the Movement, similar to the patriarchal roles they were fighting against in the first place, while their particular disadvantages and demands were ignored. Thus, the early decades of the Chicano Movement (1960s–1970s) were largely characterized by male-dominated expression and artistic creation.[12]

Just as Chicanas' participation in the Movement went for the most part unrecognized, so did their literary endeavors. For women who were taught loyalty to the family and the community, not to mention submission to a chauvinist ideology, writing about the female self and individuality became a subversive act. Chicanas were accused of betraying the political struggle by criticizing the behavior of fellow Chicanos, an accusation reminiscent of the one directed at African American women during their struggles in the Civil Rights Movement and their initial pursuit of literary careers.

During the late 1970s and early 1980s, Chicanas began a militant crusade to shift male-dominated social and literary issues to include a female and feminist-centered ideology that would better reflect the growing concerns of the women who participated in the Movement. Tired of feeling underrepresented and often excluded, Chicanas decided to concentrate on including feminist and gender issues in political class discussions and thus reconfigure the meaning of cultural and political resistance. This reconfiguration was accomplished through continued social activism and, most important of all, through the written word.

By bringing gender issues and questions of sexuality and female oppression to the forefront, Chicana writers broadened the thematic space of Chicano/a literature. In portraying and interrogating gender specific roles for women in Latina/o culture, Chicanas introduced a new dimension to the concept of resistance. The shift from a male-centered ideology emphasizing class, race, and political struggle to a female subjectivity that stressed a new politicized personal identity is best described by Angie Chabram-Dernersesian when she states that:

> Chicana[s] . . . of the 1970s and early 1980s crossed the seemingly impenetrable borders of Chicano subjectivity. They transformed the language of self-representation, visualized new ethnic configurations and subject positions, and paved the way for

contemporary Chicanas to explore other dimensions of the Chicana experience. Had it not been for the pioneering efforts of early Chicana cultural practitioners, who were often unjustly divorced by their own Raza, these developments would have been hampered.[13]

Sandra Cisneros absorbed the social upheavals and radicalism of the era during her adolescence and young adulthood as she made her way through the American educational system while emerging from a characteristically Mexican American upbringing. This distinct background nourished her creative spirit and set her on the path of what would later become a constant journey toward self-realization and cultural commitment.

Cisneros' journey begins with an intricate relation to writing that informs her literary works and lies at the core of her emergence and perseverance as a writer speaking from the *borderlands*.[14] In her search for images that capture her cultural and linguistic realities, Cisneros probes deeply into her ancestral past in order to come to terms with her own hybrid identity. The search has contributed to a richer understanding and appreciation of her life as a bilingual, bicultural woman. Yet the translation of her experience into artistic literary form reveals its share of obstacles. As Chicana writer and critic Gloria Anzaldúa points out:

> To write, to be a writer, I have to trust and believe in myself as a speaker, as a voice for the images. I have to believe that I can communicate with images and words and that I can do it well. A lack of belief in my creative abilities is a lack of belief in my total self and vice versa—I cannot separate my writing from any part of my life. It is all one.[15]

However, the long legacy of silence that has traditionally accompanied women of all cultural backgrounds often prevents recognition of the self as speaking subject and thus hinders the writing process. Roberta Rubenstein provides an interesting argument that relates to the silencing of women when she asserts that "if women are typically muted within their own culture even when they constitute a demographic majority, then women of ethnic minority groups are doubly muted. Both gender and ethnic status render them 'speechless' in patriarchy."[16] Evangelina Vigil also addresses the silencing of Latina women as double minorities by commenting that, "removed from the mainstream of American literature and barely emerging on the Hispanic literary scene, the creativity of Latina writers exists autonomously. . . . Through their works the writers affirm that, despite the double oppression that Latinas confront as women and as minorities in this country, their intellect and creativity flourish."[17]

In addition to recognizing how gender and ethnic status operate in the silencing of women, another important factor to consider in Cisneros' writing is how the specific practices of language under patriarchy function to undermine and further silence women by denying them authority as speaking subjects. Cisneros (like many women writers who preceded her) first had to break her silence and seize subjectivity by challenging gendered language practices that presuppose a male speaker. Dale Spender remarks that "men have dominated the talk; they have dominated the spoken and the written word, so that too often when we go looking for the experience of women we find that it has been swamped—sometimes to the point of invisibility—by the overweening experience of men."[18] Cisneros, therefore, often reveals a distinctly female voice in her works that disrupts the limitations of patriarchal and racial discourses. She asserts her right to become the teller of her own stories, the author of her own experiences, and the arbiter of her own bilingual, bicultural reality.

Cisneros consistently deals not only with social, gender, and linguistic constraints but also with discriminatory barriers encountered by those who form part of a minority group living in the United States. Her ongoing struggles as a "double minority" only began to succeed after many years of obliteration or neglect by literary circles. In this sense, the history of Cisneros' incursion into the literary field parallels and is informed by that of many American women writers in general, exhibiting at times the same types of complications and prejudgments.[19]

On the other hand, Cisneros' literary experience steps away from the trajectory of Anglo American women writers when issues of feminism, ethnicity, and race come to the forefront. In this respect, her writing falls in line with literature written by women of other ethnic groups (i.e., African American, Asian American, Native American) since the historical and sociopolitical conditions that influenced the formation of these writers are in many ways similar and related to one another. In an interview with Feroza Jussawalla and Reed Way Dasenbrock, Cisneros comments:

> I guess my feminism and my race are the same thing to me. They're tied in one to another, and I don't feel an alliance or an allegiance with upper-class white women. I don't. I can listen to them and on some level as a human being I can feel great compassion and friendship; but they have to move from their territory to mine, because I know their world. But they don't know mine.[20]

Because of her commitment to Latino/a social causes and her desire to disseminate the rich artistic contributions of her culture, Cisneros at times experienced racial intolerance toward Anglo Americans for what she considered a disengaged attitude regarding others' cultures. Yet with continued exposure to social activism and the literary world, she has since modified her views and feels she is in a more balanced place: "My politics have been changing, and some of my white women friends who have come into my life . . . have taught me a lot. Those white women friends who have bothered to learn about my culture have taught me something [and] a little sliver of glass of the Snow Queen in my heart has dissolved a bit. But I'm still angry about some things. . . ."[21]

Cisneros' writing also shares characteristics with postcolonial literatures in that the writing is informed by the experience of colonization. In *The Empire Writes Back: Theory and Practice in Postcolonial Literature,* Bill Ashcroft points out that "women in many societies have been relegated to the position of Other, marginalized and, in a metaphorical sense, colonized. . . . They share with colonized races and peoples an intimate experience of the politics of oppression and repression. . . ."[22] Cisneros' efforts to construct a language of her own, which in turn serves to channel her ethnic American experience transforms into a struggle "to reinstate the marginalized in the face of the dominant."[23] In this sense, Cisneros draws both on aspects of postcolonial and feminist discourses in her articulation of female experience, an articulation that motivated Jussawalla and Dasenbrock to interview Cisneros and include her, along with several others authors, in a collection titled, *Interviews with Writers of the Post-Colonial World.*[24]

From the late 1980s through the 1990s, Chicana writers, and Sandra Cisneros in particular, enjoyed more success and received more critical attention due to increasing dissemination of their works through a wider range of publishers.[25] They also experimented with innovative narrative techniques— mixing genres, languages, and styles. Many Chicanas introduced and adopted new literary forms such as the "conscious essay" (a term coined in the 1980s by Chicana writers) in which the author more directly states what is on her mind. The personal tone and direct voice of the writer characterizes these essays and positions the female as authoritative voice within the writing. Different views on race, gender, ethnicity, sexuality, and identity are reflected in this type of writing.

Examples of conscious essays, along with poetry, short stories, and sketches by ethnic women, predominantly appear in two groundbreaking works: Gloria Anzaldúa's and Cherríe Moraga's *This Bridge Called My Back: Writings By Radical Women of Color*[26] and Anzaldúa's *Making Face, Making Soul/Haciendo Caras: Creative and Critical Perspectives by Feminists of Color.*[27] The major area of concern in these two editions is the destructive and demoralizing effects of racism and sexism particularly experienced by women of color. Other concerns include the ways in which Third World women derive a feminist political theory grounded in their racial/cultural background. Contemporary writing by Chicanas and other women of color speaks more openly and directly to altering traditional gender roles and institutions that constrict or degrade female experience. Chicanas began to exert control over their lives and their sexuality while simultaneously creating artistic literary outlets that portray their collective experience. As Chabram-Dernersesian points out, "these were the Chicanas who replaced the discourses of compadres and carnalismo with the discourses of comadres [sisters] and feminismo [feminism], macho with hembra, and fiercely combated male domination in the leadership of the Chicano Movement and the political life of the community."[28] Furthermore, some Chicana writers expressed particular interest in articulating a Chicana lesbian identity in works such as Norma Alarcón's, Cherríe Moraga's, and Ana Castillo's *The Sexuality of Latinas*[29] and Carla Trujillo's *Chicana Lesbians: The Girls Our Mothers Warned Us About.*[30]

An influential issue that looms large in Sandra Cisneros' works, as well as in the works of other Latinas, is her concern over borders—social, cultural, racial, and linguistic divisions that often circumscribe and limit human inter-action and creative/artistic expression. This concern arises from her need to consolidate, understand, and constantly translate two (or more) cultures, languages, and worldviews. Cisneros remarks how Chicanas are "always strad-dling two countries, and we're always living in that kind of schizophrenia that I call being a Mexican woman living in an American society, but not belonging to either culture."[31] Yet in recent years, and largely due to Anzaldúa's impor-tant creative and critical writing, a new "*mestiza* consciousness" has emerged that addresses the issues of borders and divided loyalties. Anzaldúa defines *la mestiza* as a:

> product of the transfer of the cultural and spiritual values of one group to another. Being tricultural, mono-lingual, bilingual, or multilingual, speaking a patois, and in a state of perpetual transition, the *mestiza* faces the dilemma of the mixed breed: which collectivity does the daughter of a darkskinned mother listen to? . . . The new *mestiza* copes by developing a tolerance for contradic-tion, a tolerance for ambiguity. . . . She learns to juggle cultures. She has a plural personality. . . . The work of mestiza consciousness is to break down the subject-object duality that keeps her a prisoner and to show . . . how duality is transcended.[32]

Anzaldúa's arguments provide a means with which to reconcile and consoli-date apparently opposing cultural factors by achieving equilibrium, however tense or precarious, between two (or more) contributing races/cultures. The idea that *you need not choose* one culture over the other, that both (or all) cultures can coexist and determine your identity, that multiple subjectivities can enhance rather than hinder the creative literary process, were notions welcomed by Cisneros and other Chicana writers.[33] Stepping increasingly away from the basic precepts of social protest literature that characterized the early Chicano Movement, Cisneros began to focus her efforts on defining a new cultural and social space that reflects a growing awareness of her own voice and concerns.

Alicia Gaspar de Alba captures the essence of Cisneros' role as a writer when she states that:

> the Chicana writer, like the curandera [medicine woman] or the bruja [witch], is the keeper of the culture, keeper of the memories, the rituals, the stories, the superstitions, the language, the imagery of her Mexican heritage. She is also the one who changes the culture, the one who breeds a new language and a new lifestyle, new values, new images and rhythms, new dreams and conflicts into that heritage, making . . . a new legacy for those who have still to squeeze into legitimacy as human beings and American citizens.[34]

In this sense, as readers, we appreciate Cisneros' talents in combining the roles of historian, healer, teacher but also part creator, sociologist, activist, and constructor of a new identity that better defines her life as a contemporary Chicana, woman, and writer.

Through education, skills, training, and feminist activism, Cisneros (and other Latinas) have found ways to break through the cycles of poverty, sexism, isolation, and exclusion that have characterized past generations of women. They have also found modes of articulating (through writing and publishing) strategies to help vindicate their position as self-assertive, strong-willed agents reacting against oppressive systems of power while providing reconsiderations of traditional images and myths associated to notions of femininity. In addition, through social activism and involvement in women's causes, Cisneros and other Latinas constantly strive to become, in Blea's terms, "citizens with full legal rights and responsibilities," women charting their own destinies through engagement and commitment.[35]

Another issue Cisneros has confronted throughout her life and literary career is the debate over nomenclatures or ethnic labels. Various critical, anthropological, and demographic studies conducted throughout the years clearly demonstrate that use of the term *Latina/o* came forth with a degree of contention. Because of the amalgamation of various cultures, languages, customs, and traditions, the practice of group labeling (Hispanic, Latina/o, Chicano/a) set forth arduous debates during the late 1960s and early 1970s that, in many ways, continue to this day. Initially, U.S. governmental agencies (particularly the U.S. Census Bureau) sought to group all Spanish-speaking peoples under one identifiable rubric but failed to consider essential cultural differences among the groups' constituents. The practice of amalgamating diverse cultural groups under one umbrella label suggests two politically motivated strategies. First, the generalized term *Hispanic* promotes, according to Mary Romero, the "depoliticization of each group's history within the U.S. (colonized, conquered, exploited, etc.)."[36] Second, the term favors Hispanic/ European culture and ancestry over African and indigenous cultures as precursors of a national identity.[37]

While the label *Hispanic* emerged as a political construct initially coined by the U.S. government, most studies reveal the inadequacy of the term in designating diverse populations from various national origins. Latinas/os are physically and culturally a heterogeneous group and thus cannot be easily classified under one racial/ethnic category. Nevertheless, the question remains as to the continued use of the term *Hispanic*. If the designation is such a "politically contested" term, why does it continue to appear in the titles of many anthologies and in so many discussions on Latino/a literary studies? A possible answer to this question lies in the continued use of a common language: Spanish. Yet even when it may appear that Spanish (derived from Latin roots) is the common denominator uniting the cultural groups, deeper probing into each group's use of the language reveals marked variations depending on colloquialisms, idiomatic expressions, and other linguistic influences.

Language, then, cannot be seen as the *only* unifying force and cultural indicator of identity. Each cultural group needs to be studied individually in order to assess its growth and literary evolution. Candace Nelson and Marta Tienda remark that "while common ancestral ties to Spain manifested in language, religion, and various traditions suggest an underlying cultural commonality, the diverse incorporation experiences of Mexicans, Puerto Ricans, and Cubans have contributed to significant social and economic differences that have remained intact over time. It is this persistence of socioeconomic differentiation . . . that challenges the conception of 'Hispanic' as a coherent ethnic category. . . ."[38]

William Luis presents an alternate discussion on the issue of ethnic labeling in his influential study *Dance Between Two Cultures: Latino Caribbean Literature Written in the United States*.[39] From the very beginning of his study, Luis argues that he prefers the term *Latina/o* since it "refers to political, social, historical, and racial realities"[40] relevant to the lives of Latin American and Caribbean peoples living in the United States. Moreover, we cannot ignore other ramifications of the term summarized by Luis:

> The term Latino refers to oppressed people in the United States. It is derived by those who are colonized or oppressed within the colonial power looking out toward the neocolonial countries. . . . Latino refers to an identity postcolonial people have developed within the colonizing country—an identity that does not extend outside its geographic borders.[41]

Luis's belief that the term *Latina/o* does not extend outside geographic borders is shared by Pedro Cabán who notes that descendents from Latin America and the Caribbean prefer to identify themselves based on their country of origin when mingling with one another. Cabán states that "a Chicana, a Dominicano, and a Puertorriqueña may seek to unite as Latinos in order to confront institutionalized racism, build electoral alliances to acquire local political power, or simply gain space within an institution. But once exclusively in the company of another Latin American, we jettison 'Latino.'"[42] Marta Caminero-Santangelo also writes on the problematic issue of a defining, all-encompassing ethnic label. She offers a copious discussion in the introduction to her work *On Latinidad: U.S. Latino Literature and the Construction of Ethnicity* that considers the myriad discussions of ethnic labels by writers and scholars throughout the years.[43] She eventually decides on the following approach:

> I have chosen [after all my laborious dissection of it] to accept the category "Latino" and use it, without assuming any more fundamental connections between the various groups but in acknowledgement of the fact that a sense of a larger group identity has tentatively been constructed—often by popular culture—in the United States. . . . "Latino" allows me a certain easy [if dangerous] shorthand; but more important, it also gives me the tools for discussing how the various groups engage with dominant-culture conceptions of themselves, as well as with each other. Sometimes . . . that engagement does indeed come to look something like a forged sense of peoplehood.[44]

Sandra Cisneros herself also adds her perspective concerning the use of these controversial terms. In the interview conducted by Jussawalla and Dasenbrock, Cisneros is adamant in her opinion over contentious ethnic labels:

> I hate Hispanic. One day that word just appeared! Just like *USA Today.* One day we were sleeping, we woke up and saw that. "How'd that get there?" (Laughter) I don't know where that word came from. It's kind of an upwardly mobile type word. That word to me came out of Washington, D.C. I only use it when I apply for a grant. But something I've learned is not to feel superior when people want to call themselves Hispanic. You have a right to call yourself what you want, and I have to respect that if I want to be called what I want to be called. So, I no longer get so hysterical anymore if someone wants to call themselves that. But you wouldn't find me going out with a Hispanic. (Laughter) Anyway, we had a word, no one asked us! I like the word Latino. It groups me with the other Latino groups. . . . [45]

In conclusion, regarding the debates over nomenclatures, and after considering divergent angles of inquiry and contestation regarding this topic, perhaps it would be best to follow Caminero-Santangelo's advice at the end of her study where she proposes the following:

> What if we saw *latinidad* as a *commitment*—not just to an exploration of conditions that encourage panethnic collectivity but also to an exploration of those conditions (including differences) which potentially inhabit it? . . . The "Latino" rubric allows me to discuss those differences, paying careful attention to the divergent histories and present circumstances of different groups and the reasons for these. . . . Thus, ironically, strategically accepting the to-some-degree hegemonically constructed, homogenizing category of "Latino" allows me to understand the category's homogenizing tendencies. . . . At its best, identifying as Latina or Latino allows us to express, to ourselves and to others, our *commitment* to attending to the historical and present differences among Latinos, as well as to the sometimes overlapping or analogous histories and current structural problems—which is another way of saying our commitment to solidarity.[46]

The complex issue of cultural and racial identity has long been the subject of many critical studies and debates. However, in order to place Cisneros' writing within a larger discussion of cultural affiliations that surface as an important component of her narrative works, it is necessary to address the issues of labeling/nomenclatures and the interaction of different cultural groups with one another. The object of this discussion is not to dwell on differentiation and division but, rather, to focus on how history, culture, race, and gender inform the thematic concerns and narrative techniques characteristic to Cisneros' writing.

The primary focus of this work, then, is to chart the developmental phases of Cisneros' life and her representations of Chicana experience rooted in a particular historical, cultural, and racial context. The study examines Cisneros' background, upbringing, cultural identity, and family history and the ways in which this history influences her writing. It also considers the repercussions of her literary act (often seen as a form of "transgression") in its relation to the larger scope of American literature. The concept of transgression stems from Anzaldúa's commentary: "for silence to transform into speech, sounds and words, it must first traverse through our female bodies. For the body to give birth to utterance, the human entity must recognize itself as carnal. . . . Because our bodies have been stolen, brutalized or numbed, it is difficult to speak from/through them. . . . When she transforms silence into language, a woman transgresses."[47] Through the historical and political contexts of Anzaldúa's message, Cisneros has learned to "transgress," and her voice reverberates in ways that address her particular experience as a contemporary Chicana.

In my study of Sandra Cisneros' life and works, I follow the "*salpicón*" approach described by Tey Diana Rebolledo in *Women Singing in the Snow: A Cultural Analysis of Chicana Literature* in which she asserts that any discussion of the life and works of Latino/a authors "must be appropriate and well integrated . . . and that praxis is as important as theory."[48] In this sense, the "*salpicón*" approach consists of a more eclectic analysis rather than on the imposition of any *single* critical argument or narrative structure. I also respect Rebolledo's argument that criticism of works by Latina/o writers should come from those familiar with the historical and cultural contexts in which the works were written.

Much of my analysis relies on several sources on Cisneros' life and works. Two biographical references have been particularly helpful: Caryn Mirriam-Goldberg's *Sandra Cisneros: Latina Writer and Activist*[49] and Virginia Brackett's *A Home in the Heart: The Story of Sandra Cisneros.*[50] For socio-historical and narrative analysis related to Cisneros' works I primarily rely on the scholarship of Juan Bruce-Novoa, Gloria Anzaldúa, Norma Alarcón, Tey Diana Rebolledo, Alvina Quintana, Angie Chabram-Dernersesian, and Alicia Gaspar del Alba, among others. I also consulted a wide range of periodicals, journals, reviews, and interviews (mentioned throughout the discussion of the following chapters) as well as numerous online sources that focus on Cisneros' life, her writing, and her social activism.

In my initial research for this project, I found that there was a perceptible divide between the biographical and critical sources published on Cisneros and her works. Either the studies primarily portrayed incidents in her life with generalized glimpses into her literary/artistic production or they focused entirely on critical evaluation of her writing at the expense of including biographical details. Several references emphasized her social activism but failed to accurately foreground this activism within a Mexican American socio-historical context crucial to the understanding of Cisneros' concerns. In this sense, my work combines both Cisneros' personal and professional worlds and reveals how inextricable one is from the other and how Cisneros manages to harmonize these two often conflicting yet prevalent aspects of her existence.

In many ways, my interest in Cisneros' accomplishments and important contributions to the field of contemporary literature responds to Susan Snaider

Lanser's exhortation for more studies of women's fiction, from different cultures and vantage points, in order to "speak with authority about women writers and narrative voice."[51] I find Lanser's arguments and her interrogations into the problems of establishing a female literary voice within a patriarchal social and literary environment particularly pertinent to the study of Cisneros' and other Latinas' writing. Lanser's discussion of "communal voice" in *Fictions of Authority: Women Writers and Narrative Voice*[52] informs my analysis of Cisneros' writing. The construction of a communal voice is directly related to the formation of a distinct discourse that enables the teller(s) to control the narration of events. Cisneros' main literary interest is to create close rapport rather than rupture or distance between the storytelling agent(s) and the listeners/receptors engaged on the opposite end of the literary spectrum. This rapport, in turn, shifts the focus of attention away from individual protagonists to a more socially conscious and culturally inscribed group of characters (particularly women) ranging in age and class positions. In so doing, Cisneros generates an ideal setting for the development of a communal narrative. And this narration is intricately connected to and informed by her lived experience.

Communities of women and the need for addressing female concerns/issues emerge as constant motifs in Cisneros' texts. Whether the stories are presented through the adolescent eyes of the narrator Esperanza Cordero (*The House on Mango Street*)[53] or Lala Reyes (*Caramelo*)[54]; through the more mature voices of Rosario, Clemencia, Ines, and Lupe (*Woman Hollering Creek and Other Stories*)[55]; or through the decidedly liberated yet often controversial perspectives of her poetic personae (*My Wicked Wicked Ways,*[56] *Loose Woman*[57]), each narrator functions in relation to the community from which she learns valuable lessons and through which she develops her sense of identity.

My discussion begins by documenting Cisneros' biographical development in Chapter 1, "An Artist in the Making." This chapter includes details related to Cisneros' parents and family background; her birth, upbringing, and education; and the trips from the United States (Chicago) to Mexico (Mexico City) and vice versa that formed a crucial part of her early childhood. The discussion then turns to her experience as a student (elementary and high school, Loyola University, University of Iowa's Writers Workshop), her subsequent employments (Latino Youth Alternative High School, Loyola University, Guadalupe Cultural Arts Center, University of California, etc.), and different places of residence (Chicago; San Antonio; Chico, California; Europe, etc.). This chapter also traces the years subsidized by different grants (National Endowment for the Arts, Dobie Paisano Foundation, MacArthur Foundation) that allowed her to focus more on her writing.

Chapter 2, "Telling to Live: An Approach to Sandra Cisneros' Fictional World," explores her creative process in semiautobiographical sketches and fictionalized representations of predominantly Latina characters, experiences, and worldviews through an analysis of her first novel and her short story collection (*The House on Mango Street*; *Woman Hollering Creek and Other Stories*).

This chapter also examines the historical/cultural/linguistic contexts that gave way to Cisneros' creativity as well as the repercussions of her literary works within the larger Anglo-American and Latino/a reading audiences.

Chapter 3, "Entering into the Serpent: A Provocative Chicana Poetics," provides an analysis of Cisneros' poetry collections (*Bad Boys*; *My Wicked Wicked Ways*; *Loose Woman*) by focusing on her use of imagery and metaphor, linguistic and syntactic merging, the interrogation of social/cultural and gender constructs, and the use of innovative poetic structures. I also highlight Cisneros' distinction between prose and poetry writing as well as her approaches to both literary forms.

Chapter 4, "*Caramelo:* Weaving Family and National History into Storytelling," focuses on Cisneros' interaction with family members in recent years, particularly her relationship to her father in the year leading up to his death, while also providing an examination of Cisneros' most recent novel about a multigenerational Mexican American family largely based on her father's life story. The novel is the first of her works to be published and launched simultaneously in English and in Spanish. I explore the thematic concerns, characterizations, aesthetic use of language, notion of hybrid identities, and cultural loyalties, among other aspects of her longest literary work to date.

In Chapter 5, "A Rebellious Soul in San Antonio: Sandra Cisneros' Social Activism," I discuss the importance of Cisneros' work in academic institutions, social agencies, and the publication industry. In addition, I examine her role as social activist involved in community affairs, particularly those related to the development and improvement of Latino/a lives. This role induced her to confront the King Williams District Board of Directors in San Antonio, Texas, to exert her constitutional rights as an American citizen living on American soil yet intricately connected to her Mexican roots and cultural practices. Her interest in communities of women also led her to participate in the collaborative film project, "The Desert Is No Lady,"[58] showcasing the artistic production of Southwestern women of diverse cultural backgrounds. Finally, I will comment on Cisneros' intervention in creating the week-long Macondo Writing Workshop in San Antonio, Texas, founded in 1995, that transforms the city into a space of intense artistic and cultural creativity.

In *New Ways of Telling: Latinas' Narratives of Exile and Return,* Jacqueline Stefanko comments that "in the liminality of this moment in history, when discourses, disciplines, and politics converge and contend with one another, when border-crossing has become a site of resistance and liberatory possibilities, I see Latin American women writing in the United States mapping out paradigmatic shifts in the ways we read and write."[59] In many ways, Sandra Cisneros has redefined and broadened traditional notions of what constitutes a work of art; of the merging of histories, languages, and cultures used in the narration of these works; and the increasing acceptance and anticipation with which the texts are received by the reading public. Her literary efforts and award-winning career have transformed her into one of the most recognized, widely read, and studied authors whose works have been translated into twelve different languages. Her bilingual, bicultural life story is a significant example of steadfast perseverance and accomplishment and her literary works are meaningful contributions to a multifaceted American literary tradition. Cisneros' role as educator and social activist, along with her literary works, all combine to create one of the most assertive, outspoken, socially conscious, and groundbreaking literary voices of our time.

ONE

An Artist in the Making

You insult me
when you say I'm
schizophrenic.
My divisions are
infinite.

—Bernice Zamora, "So Not to Be Mottled"

Mexico and the United States share a long history that dates as far back as the eighteenth century. The gradual westward expansion of North Americans under the tenets of Manifest Destiny[1] initiated the first confrontations between the two nations, eventually resulting in the Mexican American War (1846–48) and the signing of the Treaty of Guadalupe Hidalgo.[2] Mexican (im)migration, however, initiated well before several territories were incorporated as states and increased during and after the Mexican Revolution (1910–17) when a large percent of Mexican citizens fled their homelands in search of safer environments, job opportunities, and economic stability. U.S. immigration laws established in the 1920s put a stop to indiscriminate entry to the United States, thus requiring Mexicans to provide proof of identity and documentation in order to enter the country.[3] Although most immigrants complied with the new regulations, others entered the country by foregoing border patrol. It was during this time, according to Himilce Novas, that "the term 'illegal immigrant' entered the American vocabulary."[4]

In the 1940s, an alternate method of legal entry for Mexicans into the United States was the Bracero Program.[5] Though the program was harshly criticized on both sides of the border for different reasons, it nonetheless provided job opportunities for millions of Mexican immigrants throughout the United States and greatly benefited the farm industry in Texas, California, Arizona, Arkansas, New Mexico, Colorado, and Michigan. Another option for Mexicans to gain U.S. citizenship and legal entry was to join the U.S. Armed Forces during World War II (1939–45). Such was the case of Sandra Cisneros' father, Alfredo Cisneros del Moral.

Alfredo came from a wealthy Mexican family background that was less economically stable by the time he was born. Always a restless spirit, Alfredo decided to try his luck in the United States after failing to pursue a college career in accounting financed by his father. Rather than confront a strong-willed and disappointed parent, Alfredo escaped to the United States, illegally crossing the U.S.–Mexico border. When he was eventually apprehended as an illegal immigrant, state authorities gave him two choices: he could either be deported and returned to Mexico or enlist and fight for the United States in World War II. Alfredo, fearful of his father's wrath and disapproval, "ran away like a prodigal son. Out of terror."[6] He became a U.S. citizen, went to war, and came back to settle permanently in the United States. His goal was to make it to California with his younger brother in tow as they had heard that there was a large Mexican population in that state. He traveled west with his brother by bus and on a routine stop in the city of Chicago they decided to get off and explore the city a little longer. The impromptu exploration turned into permanent living arrangements. Shortly afterward, Alfredo met Elvira Cordero Anguiano, his future wife.

Unlike Alfredo's family, who for the most part still lived in Mexico, Elvira's family was a composite of Mexican immigrants from a different social class. Cisneros' maternal grandfather, fleeing the onslaught of the Mexican Revolution, immigrated to the United States to work on the railroads in Chicago. He eventually managed to save enough money to send for his family. Life in the States distanced them from Mexican relatives and so Elvira grew up in a poor Mexican American neighborhood with Spanish-speaking parents, slowly assimilating the language and ways of the host country. Cisneros speaks fondly of her mother when she asserts that she was "a very feisty, strong, and independent woman. It's too bad that she was born when she was, because I think that women were nurtured so much they were made helpless. . . . On the other hand, I'm sure if it weren't for her, my brothers and I would not be the creative individuals we are. So in a sense, we're living her dreams for her."[7]

Shortly after Alfredo's arrival in Chicago, he met Elvira at a dance. She was initially turned off by his arrogant attitude and boastful descriptions of family wealth. Cisneros jokes that "my father came from a middle-class family and here he was with Chicanos. He was trying to show off. He would tell my mother all these things, how much money he made. She always said she couldn't stand him because he was such a show-off. I don't know why she married him."[8] Alfredo and Elvira settled in Chicago's north side, an area largely populated by Puerto Ricans, Mexicans, and Mexican Americans.

Sandra Cisneros was born into the family on December 20, 1954, and would eventually become the only daughter in a family of six siblings. Cisneros' sister Carolina died shortly after birth, leaving her the odd number out amongst six brothers who quickly paired off with each other. While Alfredo worked as an upholsterer to support the family, Elvira became a housewife. Cisneros recalls that, because her father and brothers expected her to follow traditional gender roles in which males were always in control, she felt at times like she had seven fathers. "I am the only daughter in a family of six sons," she once stated. "That explains everything."[9]

Though the family was permanently settled in the United States, they frequently traveled back to Mexico to visit Cisneros' paternal grandparents. She writes:

> Every couple of years we would have to pack all our things, store the furniture I don't know where, pile into the station wagon and head south to Mexico. It was usually a stay of two months, always at the grandparents' house in La Fortuna, número 12. That famous house, the only constant in a series of traumatic upheavals we experienced as children, and, no doubt, for a stubborn period of time, my father's only legitimate "home" as well.[10]

This shifting back and forth between two countries, cultures, and languages formed a pivotal part of Cisneros' early years and, to a large extent, infuses every aspect of her life and writing. During these trips she became painfully aware of her social conditioning and class position, feeling like an outsider visiting relatives in Mexico while at the same time not quite fitting into Anglo American society and culture.

Cisneros was mainly educated in Catholic parochial schools (St. Callistus and St. Alloysius) in the city of Chicago. She remembers that the shuffling back and forth between the United States and Mexico made her early years quite unsettling and consequently made her "very introverted and shy" as she comments, "I do not remember making friends easily, and I was terribly self-conscious due to the cruelty of the nuns [at St. Callistus Elementary School] who were majestic at making one feel little. Because we moved around so much, and always in neighborhoods that appeared like France after WWII— empty lots and burned-out buildings—I retreated inside myself."[11]

At St. Aloysius, however, she found a more nurturing environment and opportunities to excel academically. The Sisters of Christian Charity who founded the school encouraged her to read more when they noticed her interest in books. But Cisneros also credits her mother with instilling in her a love of reading. Because there were few books available in their home, Elvira made sure her daughter got a library card that would allow her to check books out of the neighborhood public library and develop reading habits at an early age. In an article for *Revista Mujeres*, Cisneros pays tribute to her mother's tenacious spirit:

> Because of my mother, I spent my childhood afternoons in my room reading instead of in the kitchen. . . . I never had to change my little brother's diapers, I never had to cook a meal alone, nor was I ever sent to do laundry. Certainly I had my share of housework to do as we all did, but I don't recall it interfering with my homework or my reading habits.[12]

And so, Cisneros claims, that she is "here today because my mother let me stay in my room reading and studying, perhaps because she didn't want me to inherit her sadness and her rolling pin."[13] Elvira's love for books, libraries, museums, and public concerts was instilled in her children who were able to rise from their economically disadvantaged condition to become professionals in their own right. Aside from her literary career, Cisneros counts among her siblings a doctor, an artist, a musician, a geologist, and business owners. And although Elvira was not an educated woman (she never finished ninth grade), she was a self-made woman who followed and debated the arguments of renowned author and radio/television personality Studs Terkel as well as educator/linguistic theorist Noam Chomsky, among others.

The encouragement Cisneros received to pursue reading came hand in hand with the family's move to its first home on North Campbell Avenue, in Humboldt Park (Chicago). Cisneros described the new house in the following terms:

> It was an ugly little house, bright red as if it was holding its breath, a small two-story bungalow in a Puerto Rican neighborhood on the north side. This move to a permanent home ended our nomadic existence for a while, and this was important not only for my emotional security, but because it placed me in a neighborhood, a real one, with plenty of friends and neighbors that would evolve into the eccentric characters of *The House on Mango Street*.[14]

Though the new house was far from the image she envisioned, it provided Cisneros, for the first time and at the age of twelve, with a room of her own and gave the family a sense of permanence that was absent from former years of shifting from one rented apartment to another. Previously, Cisneros had to share rooms with her siblings or any other visitors in cramped quarters, which often meant a sleeping cot in the middle of the living room. Her own room now gave her the much-needed space she craved for reading and writing. Since her brothers bonded closely together, excluding her from their inner circle, and since she lost the only sister she had during her childhood, Cisneros turned to books for solace and thus escaped her isolation. Years later she admits, "had my sister lived or had we stayed in one neighborhood long enough for a friendship to be established, I might not have needed to bury myself in books the way I did."[15]

Cisneros' first access to books came from the limited choices of her home and school library. The Cisneros family owned only two books in its household: a Catholic Bible and an old copy of Lewis Carroll's *Alice in Wonder-land*. Her elementary school teachers encouraged her to read, but the school library did not have many alternatives. Cisneros points out that "[s]ince our school was poor, so were the choices. As a result, I read a lot of books I might not have read otherwise; the lives of saints, or very stodgy editions of children's stories published in the 1890s—usually didactic, Horatio Alger-type tales which I enjoyed all the same because of the curious English."[16] She relied more and more on her public library card for books.

Early on, Cisneros classified the reading materials she was exposed to by noticing that there were two types of books:

> There were the books of school that were not very interesting at all, and there were the books in the library that were so wonderful you could begin reading them in the daytime and not even notice when the dark came. It was the latter group that became my companions in the solitary wreckage of homes we lived in. I remember being so immersed in my books that my life began to take on a romantic narrator and I was the story's main character. I began narrating all my waking hours and would tag "he said's" and "she said's" to the tail of all sentences directed to me.[17]

The books she enjoyed the most and the ones she checked out over and over again were mainly fairy tales and adventure stories: Hugh Lofting's *Doctor Doolittle* series; *The Island of the Blue Dolphins; Hittie: Her First 100 Years; Through the Looking Glass; Six Swans,* among others. Yet the book that most captured her attention and imagination during her childhood years was Virginia Lee Burton's *The Little House.* Focused on the story of a great grand-daughter who saves a house she inherits from the increasing industrialization that surrounds it, Cisneros pondered over the analogies between *The Little House* and her own house and concluded that the great granddaughter's efforts to preserve a cherished home space paralleled her own: "*The Little House* was my own dream. And I was to dream myself over again in several books, to re-invent my world according to my own vision."[18]

Cisneros' vision, fueled by her childhood reading, further developed when she began her freshman year at Josephinum High School, an all-girls Catholic school, in 1968. Though she claimed to have written her first poem at the age of ten, Cisneros began to take writing more seriously as a teenager. Encouraged to write more by one of her teachers, she eventually became editor of the school literary magazine and published some of her first poems. Her continued isolation from social circles, especially the young dating scene in her school, prompted her into the realm of reading and writing, though, she admits, she "was ready to sacrifice everything in the name of love, to do anything, even risk my own life, but thankfully there were no takers."[19]

After high school graduation, Cisneros enrolled in the English Department at Loyola University (a Jesuit institution in Chicago) in 1972 with a scholarship she earned to pursue a college degree. She was the only Chicana enrolled at the time in the English Department. As a second-generation Mexican

American, a college education was an unusual path for Cisneros to follow in the patriarchal upbringing in which she was raised. To her surprise, her father was immediately pleased with the prospect of her future studies, though she did not know at the time that Alfredo Cisneros' view of college was a step in the direction to finding a respectable husband. Cisneros comments:

> Being only a daughter for my father meant that my destiny would lead to become someone's wife. . . . In retrospect . . . I'm lucky that my father believed daughters were meant for husbands. It meant it didn't matter if I majored in something silly like English. After all, I'd find a nice professional, right? This allowed me the liberty to putter about embroidering my little poems and stories without my father interrupting . . . .[20]

Cisneros continued to nurture her passion for writing and during her junior year at Loyola she enrolled in her first writing workshop. The class required that she share her writing with other classmates, exchange and receive critical reviews, as well as edit/revise her poems on a weekly basis. It was the first formal and rigorous experience with writing at the college level. With this experience also came a broadened notion of literary works and authors. What she slowly began to notice, however, was the absence of any writers or scenes she could relate to on a personal level. Exposed to the literary canon and most reputable works in her courses on American literature, she rarely came across any voices that reflected the people and daily events of her neighborhood and lived experience. The closest she came to connecting with any author was when she read the poetry of Emily Dickinson. "I like to think of that extraordinary woman," Cisneros said, "who in her later life never even strayed beyond the house and its gardens, but who wrote in her lifetime 1,775 poems. . . . She gave me inspiration and hope."[21] Yet what she soon realized was that, despite her love for Dickinson's poetry, there were essential differences between their lives, namely Dickinson's access to education, her class position, and her inherited wealth. This realization prompted Cisneros to question the underpinnings of racial and class privilege that were increasingly absent from her bicultural surroundings.

As she continued to read and write, Cisneros began to create a distinct voice of her own that she had been unconsciously nurturing for years. It began in her childhood years and her first exposure to literature. She constantly juxtaposed scenes or conversations from her daily life with a creative narrative voice:

> "I want you to go to the store and get me a loaf of bread and a gallon of milk. Bring back all the change and don't let them gyp you like they did last time." In my head my narrator would add: . . . *she said in a voice that was neither reproachful nor tender. Thus clutching the coins in her pocket, our hero was off under a sky so blue and a wind so sweet she wondered it didn't make her dizzy.*[22]

Cisneros also started to merge the voices she heard at home and in her neighborhood with the imaginary voice she created in her head. So she relied on her mother's English acquired in the Mexican American neighborhoods of her youth and on her father's Spanish, influenced by his Mexican upbringing. According to Cisneros, "these two voices at odds with each other—my mother's punch-you-in-the-nose English and my father's powdered-sugar Spanish—curiously are the voices that surface in my writing."[23]

Cisneros' creative narrative voice was further enhanced by her exposure to the works of poets Donald Justice, James Wright, and Mark Strand, among others, who, according to Eduardo Elías, "had influenced a whole generation of Spanish writers, thus bringing Cisneros into touch with her cultural roots."[24] Upon graduating from Loyola University in 1976, and following the advice of supportive teachers, Cisneros enrolled in the Master of Fine Arts Program in Creative Writing at the University of Iowa, moving away for the first time from her home and neighborhood. Doubting whether she would ever be admitted, and unaware that she was applying to one of the most prestigious writing programs at the university level, Cisneros was surprised to discover that she had been accepted from among the many applicants to the institution. However, her desires to study and write under the tutelage of poet Donald Justice, who also taught at the University of Iowa at the time, quickly vanished when she found out that he was on a sabbatical leave working on his own research project.

Cisneros soon realized that the academic and social environment found in the graduate program was very different from the one she left behind in Chicago during her formative years. Race and class issues came to the forefront as she saw that the majority of the students enrolled in the program were white, middle- to upper-class, "cultivated in the finest schools of the country like hot house orchids," which immediately made her question, "what could I write about that they couldn't? What did I know that they didn't?"[25] Cisneros' quest for answers to these questions took her on a journey of self-discovery and cultural affirmation that she had hitherto disregarded as valuable subject matter for her writing. Though Cisneros acknowledges the trials and tribulations set forth by the program (staunch competition, impelling due dates, pressure to produce, etc.), she also admits how she benefited from the experience. As Elías points out, "she had her share and fill of intimidating teachers and colleagues as well as some marvelous ones who helped and encouraged her. This was a time for Cisneros to mature emotionally, something she had neglected to do for some years—always having considered herself as somebody's daughter, lover, or friend."[26]

Joy Harjo, a Native American from Oklahoma, who had grown up on a reservation, was one of the people with whom Cisneros became close friends at the Iowa Writers Workshop. The two young women bonded with each other through their sense of isolation and difference from the rest of the students in the program. Both had distinct stories to tell, from different cultural upbringings immersed in different linguistic codes. The workshop brought them together and they supported each other's writing in ways that have left a lasting imprint on their relationship. Cisneros comments on what it meant to befriend Harjo during those tumultuous years:

> When I look back at the workshop and see who's still writing, the two of us who sat at the back of the room, frightened are the ones who are publishing—Joy Harjo and I. We were so terrified that we used to think that maybe we should get a drink before class! When I see Joy now, I say "You always had the courage to follow your intuition because you knew that was right." I could have gone either way and learned that logical, linear way to write and let go the one I had. I'm really glad she was there for that support and guidance.[27]

Another important figure Cisneros met during this time was Dennis Mathis, a young fiction writer, who would later become her editor and help her gather and assemble her stories for publication. She also found inspiration in the life and works of other women of color writers she read and studied (such as Maxine Hong Kingston and Toni Morrison) and some of the few published Chicano authors of the time (such as Gary Soto). Finally, there was also the International Writers Workshop that she frequented for its array of multicultural students from different parts of the globe (the Philippines, Argentina, Peru, Columbia, even as far as Yugoslavia) whose parties, dancing, humor, conversations, and close-knit friendly relations helped her get through the stiffness and unusual detachment of her first year in the program.

Cisneros' moment of epiphany at the Iowa's Writers Workshop is well-known and often commented on in interviews and biographical and literary articles. During a seminar titled "On Memory and the Imagination," Cisneros sat in silence as she heard her professor and classmates discuss the metaphor of a house after reading Gaston Bachelard's *Poetics of Space*.[28] Bachelard's work focuses on how our perceptions of houses and other shelters shape our thoughts, memories, and dreams. So when Cisneros began to hear her fellow classmates' accounts of two-story houses surrounded by white picket fences, of lawns and backyards, of individual experiences in spacious rooms, it became increasingly clear to her that she could not share in the same re-creation of images. "What did I know except third floor flats," she questioned.[29] In her efforts to move "farthest away from the pretty pastel syllables of my classmates," Cisneros concentrated on "smashing poetic pedestals. My joy was to create a rag-tag music from the broken-glass and tin-can speech of my childhood."[30] And these were precisely the images she chose to write about: "third-floor flats, and fear of rats, and drunk husbands sending rocks through windows, anything as far from the poetic as possible."[31] Up to this point, it hadn't occurred to her that the images of her childhood and the stories of the people who shared her upbringing had any space on the printed page. She acknowledges that until she confronted the metaphor of home space and its direct relation to the life of a young bilingual, bicultural Mexican American female raised in the poor inner-city neighborhoods of Chicago, she could not really come into her own as a storyteller and writer. As Cisneros concludes, "this is when I discovered the voice I had been suppressing all along without realizing it."[32]

With this new-found realization, Cisneros probed deeply into her past and into the life stories of the people with whom she had interacted. She recalled stories of the marginalized and scared, of the discriminated poor, of the women living under patriarchal gender codes, of her parents and siblings, of her commutes back and forth between the United States and Mexico, of her interplay with languages. She also brought to light the poetic and narrative voices she had been harboring for so many years, the voices that added a touch of imagination to her mundane activities, the child's inquisitive yet incisive voice of anxiety, fear, and shame but also of hope, love, and solidarity. Caryn Mirriam-Goldberg comments that "the simple language and vivid descriptions of where she lived enabled her to speak to and for millions of others who also grew up not knowing what having a house meant. But those she spoke for did experience surprising acts of kindness from the drunks in the neighborhood or the fragile beauty of morning glories climbing the walls of run-down buildings."[33] The more she wrote, the more she honed this voice into a persona that filtered the struggles of growing up Latina in the United States and the perpetual balancing act produced by subsisting in two worlds with two cultures, two languages, two histories. This is the narrative voice she eventually relies on during the later half of her participation in the Iowa Writers Workshop and in her first major publication, *The House on Mango Street*.[34]

In May 1978, Cisneros graduated from the University of Iowa at the age of twenty-four with a Master of Fine Arts degree in creative writing. She returned to Chicago, degree in hand, eager to further develop her writing skills and share her educational experience with others. Yet the financial responsibilities of supporting herself quickly led her in a different direction. She accepted a position at the Latino Youth Alternative High School in Chicago where she served in different capacities: initially as part-time teacher, later as arts coordinator, editor, counselor, interim director, disciplinarian, and even sometime-janitor. The school, founded in 1973, still operates as a nonprofit organization working to provide quality education for inner-city children, youth, and adults. In addition, the institution works as an effective advocate for community-based services in which the people involved are active participants in developing and running programs, not just passive recipients of services. Of her years of service at the Latino Youth Alternative High School, Cisneros comments:

> It is hard for me to describe my employment at Latino Youth. It was chaotic and ridiculous, and revolutionary, and rewarding, and tumultuous, all at once. The staff I worked with were a dedicated group of characters, eccentrics left over from the sixties, idealists and anarchists, romantics and realists. I must have seemed very fluffy indeed. But we did have in common one thing. We cared very much for the kids no matter how disparate our ideologies, or lack of.[35]

The atmosphere that Cisneros found at the Latino Youth Alternative High School was completely different from the one she experienced in Iowa. Here, the student population came from a variety of dysfunctional homes and violent surroundings. Most of them had dropped out of school, used drugs or alcohol, suffered abusive family relationships, and/or witnessed drive-by shootings. Some were already teenage parents of one or multiple children. They were plagued by low self-esteem and had difficulty socializing with others. Most of all, they believed they had few, if any, opportunities of getting ahead in life, much less of leaving their barrios.

Cisneros listened to their stories of violence, poverty, discrimination, and abuse with empathy as she absorbed their tales of human suffering. Much of her interaction with and connection to these inner-city youths would later translate into the material for her first publications. Though working at the Alternative High School for three years drained her energies and left little time for writing, Cisneros admits that "from this experience of listening to young Latinos whose problems were so great, I felt helpless; I was moved to do something to change their lives, ours, mine."[36] Her response was to put their stories down in writing within the limited time she had after working hours. Cisneros realized that, though her students had overcome dire circumstances and situations "that would have made [her] Iowa Writers Workshop classmates faint," these students were also "streetwise and savvy; they were ingenuous and fragile. They had seen troubles the world's heads of state would never see . . . and nobody had told them their lives were extraordinary. . . ."[37] Cisneros' writing became a tribute to her students' tenacious spirit and endurance despite the circumstances in which they lived. Her goal was to acknowledge that "their lives were extraordinary, that they were extraordinary for having survived," and concluded that they "held doctorates from the university of life."[38]

During the time she worked for the Latino Youth Alternative High School, Cisneros also gave poetry readings in public spaces and local coffeehouses. This gave her writing added exposure and also served as a means to relieve some of the tension brought about by her work with troubled youths. The community came to know her as a result of these readings. She soon caught the attention of the Poetry Society of America, which had recently started a poetry project funded in part by the Chicago Transit Authority and the Illinois Arts Council. The project, known as Poetry-on-the-Bus Series, consisted of collecting the works of different poets across the country and displaying their words on billboards inside city trains and buses. Cisneros' poetry was featured alongside distinguished American poets such as Carl Sandburg and Gwendolyn Brooks, among others. Her poetry also caught the eye of fellow Chicano poet Gary Soto who recognized Cisneros as one of the new voices of the Chicano/a poetic scene and helped her publish her first chapbook, *Bad Boys*, in 1980. The book, a small collection of seven poems printed by Mango Press, in San José, California, provided a glimpse into her Mexican American barrio with detailed precision and imagery. Though less than 1,000 copies were printed, it won Cisneros increased recognition and its publication gave her the added confidence to pursue her writing with a heightened sense of purpose.

Though very few copies of the original edition exist and the book is currently out of print, Cisneros included the poems in a subsequent collection of poetry titled *My Wicked Wicked Ways*.[39]

After several years of overload and responsibilities at the Latino Youth Alternative High School, Cisneros decided to move on and accepted a new position at her former alma mater, Loyola University. She worked as an administrative assistant recruiting low-income and minority students into programs at the university. She frequently went to inner-city neighborhoods to talk to Latino/a teenagers, often low-income and educationally disadvantaged students, about the possibilities of obtaining a college degree. The fact that she was a bilingual Latina, and came from the same barrio as many of these teenagers did, helped her get through to otherwise distrustful teens and parents who were usually not exposed to conversations about higher education. They received her, listened to what she had to say, and felt comfortable enough to accept her guidance and counsel. Nevertheless, Cisneros knew that the number of students who would actually take up her offer was far from the one she hoped for. The conditions of poverty and lack of family support usually prevented them from pursuing a college degree. This was especially the case for the young women in the barrio who were often raised with the alternatives of marriage and motherhood as the only models to follow.

Her work at the Latino Youth Alternative High School and her role as administrative assistant/recruiter for Loyola University exposed Cisneros to instances of social injustice and racial discrimination that plagued the lives of many Latinos/as who, like herself, dreamed of getting ahead. The idealism of the American Dream was very much a part of their lives, though many did not know what steps to take in the direction of fulfilling their aspirations. Cisneros felt much frustration and anger spurred by memories of her childhood years that also developed throughout her academic experience at the undergraduate and graduate levels. She began to question the parameters of the American Dream and its apparent inaccessibility to those who had a similar upbringing as hers.

While she continued to struggle to support herself financially, she also poured her energies into writing. The sketches she began in the writing program at the University of Iowa gave way to more written portrayals of characters caught up in similar circumstances and struggling with the same conditions as those she saw in her immediate surroundings. The naïve yet incisive adolescent narrative voice she originally cultivated in her writing was now developed into a full-fledged storytelling voice that captured the nuances and subtleties of barrio life. Once again Cisneros would rely on the familiarity of situations, people, places, and bilingual voices as subject matter for her writing. As Robin Ganz points out, Cisneros speaks in languages "as rich and diverse as the expanse they embody—they are the expressions of her immediate family, of the Chicano-Riqueño community she grew up in, and the voices from her life both between and as a part of the two cultures in which she now dwells."[40]

Thus began Cisneros' formal incursion into writing. With the help of her editor and friend Dennis Mathis and the initial encouragement of Nicolás Kanellos, founder and editor of Arte Público Press, Cisneros worked her separate yet interconnected literary pieces into what eventually became her first work of fiction, *The House on Mango Street*. Cisneros, not realizing it at the time, was on her way to becoming one of the most significant and widely read Latinas whose stories would reach an eager reading public that accepted and celebrated her work and her gift for memorable storytelling and poetic imagery.

TWO

Telling to Live:
An Approach to Sandra
Cisneros' Fictional World

Those *recuerdos* of long ago keep me mindful of listening and hearing those who
hide secrets when they tell. As a cartographer of recollection . . . I pledge to hear,
to believe them when they speak.

—Josie Méndez-Negrete,
Las Hijas de Juan: Daughters Betrayed

Sandra Cisneros' initial incursion into writing began with poetry. Her individuality as well as her awareness of a communal connection to her surroundings and to the people who shared her life made her realize that she
had something to write about, something to say. She also realized that what she
wrote about needed to flow through her bilingual, bicultural consciousness
out into the world. Her first publication was, in fact, a small chapbook of
poetry titled *Bad Boys* (published by Mango Press in 1980).[1] However, it is
really through her fiction that Cisneros first gained significant notoriety in the
publishing world.

Literary recognition began with her submission of a small sketch titled
"Chanclas" to the founder and editor, Nicolás Kanellos, of Arte Público Press
and the literary magazine, *Revista Chicano-Riqueña* (later called *The Americas
Review*), for a children's literature issue. Impressed by the short piece, Kanellos encouraged her to send more and supported the idea of working on a compilation of her stories for publication. Cisneros already had a significant
number of vignettes written and collected during the years prior to meeting

Kanellos, but she continued to struggle financially and still had a difficult time trying to focus entirely on writing. Her economic situation improved in 1982 when Cisneros received her first grant from the National Endowment for the Arts (NEA). The NEA's mission to enrich the nation's diverse cultural heritage by supporting works of artistic excellence, advancing learning in the arts, and strengthening the arts in communities throughout the country, provided valuable time for writing that Cisneros had yearned for. Though she still had to complete her work contract at Loyola University and several writing projects, the grant gave her the leisure to explore her fictional world in depth.

An important step toward more commitment to her writing came with her decision to leave Chicago. With the NEA grant money in hand and determined to focus entirely on her literary career, Cisneros moved to Provincetown, Massachusetts. Her move was also influenced by the fact that her friend, Dennis Mathis, lived close by and had agreed to provide feedback and editorial advice on her writing. Though she began to write her first sketches in 1977 at the University of Iowa's Writers Workshop, the bulk of the vignettes that would later form part of her first novel, The House on Mango Street, were created between 1979 and 1981 while she lived in Chicago and later in Provincetown. She admits that when she first began writing in graduate school she was "just writing stories more or less about people I remembered. My intent was simply to chronicle, to write about something my classmates couldn't. In a sense, I was being defensive and rebellious. In this direction to move as far away from the style of my classmates, I found a voice that was uniquely mine."[2] Her initial goal to chronicle the lives of Latinos/as in the barrio was broadened by her subsequent work experience (Latino Youth Alternative High School and Loyola University) and an increasing social consciousness that infused her writing with critical, analytical, and in some instances political overtones.

On the date of her manuscript's final submission, Cisneros asked for more time and escaped to Greece with the remainder of her NEA grant money. She kept writing, editing, and revising before she sent the final chapters. She claims to have finished writing them at 4 AM on the same day of her second deadline for submission (November 30, 1982). Almost two more years of revisions followed until Kanellos compiled the final version into the first edition of The House on Mango Street, published in 1984. By 1987 the book had already gone into its third printing. Regarding her work, Cisneros comments, "I never knew when I mailed the final stories to Nick from Athens what I had created exactly. Writing Mango Street had been like creating a quilt by the light of a flashlight. I had been sending the stories to Nick as I wrote them, and although I had some idea as to the whole I was aiming for, I wasn't sure I had produced what I had planned."[3] Nevertheless, she admits that "if The House on Mango Street has brought me anything, I'm grateful for the luxury now of writing and knowing someone out there is listening."[4]

From the very beginning The House on Mango Street[5] received rave reviews and is considered one of her most widely read works to date. It has been translated into twelve different languages and is required reading in many middle schools, high schools, and universities across the country. More than 2,000,000 copies since its initial publication have been sold and thousands of articles and literary studies have been conducted on Cisneros' work. A new, twenty-fifth anniversary edition was released in spring 2009 with a new introduction written by the author. This edition will also take her on a presentation tour, which includes appearances in St. Louis, Chicago, Kansas, Minneapolis, and New York City. Indeed, Cisneros has scheduled presentations, conferences, and events until April 2010, both in various cities in the United States and international locations such as Mexico, Spain, and Canada, among others.

The House on Mango Street initially posed a problem for critics and their reviews. Considerable debate arose regarding literary format: what *is* this work? Did Cisneros write a novel, a collection of short stories, or random sketches? Is it autobiographical, semi-autobiographical, or entirely fictional? What reading audience was the author aiming for: children, teens, university students, adults, or parents? In an interview with Carlos Queirós, Cisneros commented that she wrote the book "so that it would be approachable for all people, whether they were educated or not, and whether they were children or adults. My idea was to write it in a way that it would not make anyone feel intimidated, but welcome. I had in mind a book that would be understood and appreciated by all readers, whether a working-class person, a child, poet, literature student, writer, or bus driver. So I came from that angle of being inclusive."[6]

Gary Soto described the work as "poetic prose . . . but foremost a storytelling . . . intrinsically narrative, but not large meandering paragraphs. She writes deftly, with skill and idea, in the 'show-me-don't-tell-me' vein."[7] Penelope Mesic saw the work as "vignettes of autobiographical fiction written in a loose and deliberately simple style, halfway between a prose poem and the awkwardness of semiliteracy."[8] Cisneros herself also admitted that, in conceiving *Mango Street,* she "wanted to write a collection which could be read at any random point without having any knowledge of what came before or after. Or that could be read as a series to tell one big story. I wanted stories like poems, compact and lyrical and ending with reverberation."[9]

Cisneros' writing defies literary classification. The overlapping literary modes found in her work (poetry and prose) as well as the interconnectedness between languages (Spanish and English) are deliberately used to help her express and come to terms with her development as a writer. In addition, by incorporating Spanish dialect, impressionistic metaphor, and social commentary as well as by addressing issues such as poverty, cultural suppression, and gender roles, Cisneros reveals the uniqueness of her experience as a Chicana and her relationship to community. Through her writing, she also communicates the possibility of overcoming stereotypical portrayals of women and the inevitable clash between Mexican and American cultures.

One of the most innovative aspects of Cisneros' writing, in this and other works, is precisely the development of female characters that confront hegemonic, culturally inscribed gender roles. The predominant image of docile, submissive, nurturing, and effacing women who relegate their own needs and personal desires to tend to needs of others, particularly the men and children in their families, gives way to literary representations of assertive, self-supporting, tenacious, and strong-willed women who assume control of their lives and circumstances. The fragmented, nonlinear, unconventional structure of her work provides a means with which to express and reconcile this multi-faceted characterization and shows how the literary construction of a new mode of gendered experience always involves alteration and change. Cisneros' writing, then, presents a challenge to stylistic and aesthetic "borders" in the literary representation of female experience.

A less complicated discussion emerges regarding the role of the narrator in Cisneros' text. A distinct female voice rings through the entire narration of *Mango Street*. Esperanza Cordero, a Mexican American adolescent girl, serves both as the agent who sees and the agent who narrates. Esperanza not only performs as a participating agent within the stories she tells but also, at times, steps away from the action to focus on individual characters who make up the stories. In this sense, she is at once participant, observer, and transcriber. These multiple roles give her character the credibility of immediate, first-hand observation and place her as the primary source through which the reader receives the tales. Although her narration originates from her perceptions as an adolescent girl, the narrative reveals a maturation process as Esperanza gradually discovers her place within the larger scope of community life on Mango Street. This discovery is directly related to her development as a writer/artist. Taken as a whole, the work can be seen as Esperanza's coming-of-age story, a *bildungroman* of sorts. Yet the narrator's naïve perspective should not be mistaken as superfluous. Alvina Quintana points out that, "Although cast as naïve, the narrators themselves accentuate a sophisticated authorial intervention that challenges and resists the myth of the American 'melting-pot.' These are not simply female rite-of-passage narratives, but rather stories that reveal the complex relationships between race, class, and gender in an American context."[10]

While Cisneros' work includes portrayals of women in adverse situations (trapped, isolated, abused), the work also presents a young heroine who learns from the women caught in these situations and, at the same time, transcends to a different level of personal and social awareness. Esperanza perceives the repetitive patterns of abuse, neglect, personal unfulfillment, and isolation suffered by the women on Mango Street. Yet she does not internalize the encoded message that comes with these repetitive patterns. As Annie Eysturoy points out, Cisneros "gives voice to the ordinary experience of a young Chicana by letting Esperanza tell her own coming-of-age story, thus articulating the subjective experiences of the female 'I' who resists entrapment within sociocultural norms and expectations."[11] The literary development of this subjective characterization can be seen within the context of the socio-historical changes brought about by Second Wave Feminism[12] and a new realization of the empowerment of women in American society.

Cisneros' writing, and to a large extent the beginning of her social activism (which I will highlight in the following chapters), clearly illustrates the emergence of a feminist consciousness, a particular mindset and rhetoric rooted in previous struggles within the Civil Rights and the Women's Movements of the 1960s and 1970s. Riding on the combined efforts of many sorts of activists and on the important accomplishments of Second Wave Feminists and the Civil Rights Act that particularly benefitted women,[13] Cisneros came of age at a time when revolutionary change was still in the air. Her works constantly challenge the parameters of sexism and gender bias as well as the inequality and double standards women confronted in patriarchal society, within not only the North American social context but also her own Mexican culture and upbringing. Indeed, one of the greatest accomplishments of Cisneros' narrator in *Mango Street* (and to a large extent of Cisneros herself) is the balancing act she performs, straddling two cultures, languages, and histories, placing herself within the crux of her community while at the same time maintaining a sense of individuality and control.

Cisneros' intention in presenting the realities of barrio life and the negative effects of the social conditions experienced there contrasts with other literary portrayals that tried to "make our barrios look like Sesame Street, or some place really warm and beautiful."[14] Cisneros criticized that it may be "nice to visit a poor neighborhood, but if you have to live there every day, and deal with garbage that doesn't get picked up, and kids getting shot in your backyard, and people running through your gangway at night, and rats and poor housing. . . . It looses its charm real quick!"[15] This criticism can also be traced in Esperanza's character, which makes her life on Mango Street all the more challenging and the balancing act she performs all the more courageous.

Three main issues preoccupy Esperanza as the narrator from whose perspective the events of the story unfold: her identity, her surroundings, and her emotional release through writing.[16] Early in the work, Esperanza expresses her discontent with her name in defining her identity:

> In English my name means hope. In Spanish it means too many letters. It means sadness, it means waiting. . . . It was my great-grandmother's name and now it is mine. . . . She looked out the window all her life, the way so many women sit their sadness on an elbow. . . . I have inherited her name, but I don't want to inherit her place by the window.[17]

With the story of Esperanza's naming, Cisneros points to one of the emblematic cultural traits related to women in the Mexican American community: the encoded lesson of female submissiveness often passed down from one generation to the next. Esperanza describes her great-grandmother as "a wild horse of a woman, so wild she wouldn't marry" yet who was forcibly carried away by her great-grandfather "like a fancy chandelier" (11). By remembering her great-grandmother's sadness as she sat by the window, Esperanza gains insight into the encoded lesson regarding her name, which she inherited from her great-grandmother, yet revises its significance. Though she "would've liked to have known her [great-grandmother]," Esperanza does not "want to inherit her place by the window" (11). Consequently, Esperanza searches for an identity outside of confining patterns of domination that only offer her "sadness" and "waiting." As Julián Olivares remarks, "in the endeavor to establish her identity, to fit into her name, Esperanza also undertakes a personal quest to liberate herself from the gender constraints of her culture."[18] The section titled "My Name" ends with her desire to adopt a new name in an attempt to change her own destiny and move away from the constraints inherent in the Spanish meaning of Esperanza:

> I would like to baptize myself under a new name, a name more like the real me, the one nobody sees. Esperanza as Lisandra or Maritza or Zeze the X. Yes. Zeze the X will do. (11)

Esperanza's desire to baptize herself under a new name reveals how she rejects cultural imposition and the suppression of female self-identity. This rebellious attitude characterizes Esperanza's increasingly assertive and nonconformist stance throughout the work. It also sheds light on her role as narrator: hers will be a story of resistance and change. In fact, in an interview with Renee H. Shea, Cisneros proposed an alternate approach to the work that has since taken on new critical dimensions when she urged the reader to:

> imagine a writer in her 20s trying to find out what she wants to be. She's trying to find a political consciousness, and she's just discovering that she is "other." The book [*Mango Street*] is about the author discovering her political consciousness, not Esperanza at 12 or 13. I am searching through her for my political ideology. I was too young a writer to make her a medical student or a famous botanist, so I said, "I'll just make her an artist," not realizing that people would think she was me. Then I realized all along she was a sibyl. She said things that would come true in my life. . . . By the time the book ends, Esperanza finds a solution, but I didn't know where it was going to take me as I was writing, nor did I realize that the text itself was going to be my "home in the heart."[19]

Furthermore, the fact that the narrator links her plight to that of other women of color and cultural groups in her statement "the Chinese, like the Mexicans, don't like their women strong" (10) also suggests cross-cultural similarities in the ways in which the writers engage with racial and gender concerns in their works. Interestingly, Quintana points out that Cisneros was actually influenced by Chinese American writer Maxine Hong Kingston's story "No Name Woman"[20] in writing this particular chapter in *Mango Street* and that this inspiration "speaks to the literary alliance . . . that subverts inter-ethnic borders and boundaries."[21] In this sense, both Cisneros and Kingston may also be participating in a type of Third Wave Feminism that denounces the lack of attention to distinctions among women due to race, class, and ethnicity, thus emphasizing "identity," particularly in the case of women of color, as a site of gender struggle and resistance.[22]

Another key element of concern for the narrator Esperanza is the space she inhabits. Though she longs for a room of her own and a house she can be proud of, Esperanza and her family constantly move from one dilapidated neighborhood to another one. Even when the father finally saves enough money to purchase a house, it is far from the one the family envisioned. Esperanza links the houses her family has lived in to a sense of degradation as if the tight steps, crumbling bricks, and small windows were emblematic of her impoverished condition. Bonnie TuSmith accurately points out that "the house on Mango Street can be seen as an 'ethnic sign' that can easily close off the future for the young protagonist. . . . If she accepts it as her lot in life, then she is conforming to the dominant culture's definition of who she is. Her refusal to accept this house as home, however, indicates that she has the capacity to look beyond her present condition and continue to dream."[23] Esperanza's dreams and illusions of a real home come forth in one of the most poetically evocative sections of the work in which Cisneros combines rhythm, rhyme, alliteration, and similes to demonstrate Esperanza's yearning for a new space:

> A house of my own. Not a flat. Not an apartment in back. Not a daddy's. A house all my own. With my porch and my pillow, my pretty purple petunias. My books and my stories. . . . Only a house quiet as snow, a space for myself to go, clean as paper before the poem. (108)

In many ways, Esperanza's desire for a house that better captures her intrinsic sense of a home parallels Cisneros' personal convictions of home space. Cisneros comments that in the past she "used to be ashamed to take anyone . . . to my house because if they saw that house they would equate the house with me and my values. And I know that house didn't define me; they just saw the outside. They couldn't see what was inside. I wrote a poem that was a precursor, or perhaps the same story—about an apartment, a flat. I wrote it for the [Iowa Writers] workshop after the experience of being in that seminar ["On Memory and the Imagination"], and *House on Mango Street* began that night, that same night. I can't tell you whether the poems came first or the stories; they all came like a deluge."[24]

Unable to adapt to the harsh environment that surrounds her, Esperanza also dreams of leaving Mango Street behind, of escaping the neighborhood's limitations. Esperanza's critical eye notices all too well the fate of the women who decide to stay within the confines of Mango Street. As narrator she examines the choices they make and considers the consequences of their actions. The women often opt for marriage at an early age over education (Sally); become abandoned mothers with a house full of children (Rosa Vargas); feel out of place and grieve over memories of a previous home

(Mamacita); remain imprisoned in an apartment by a jealous husband (Rafaela); or end up victims of repeated domestic violence (Minerva). Yet it is precisely through these women that Esperanza begins to understand and come to terms with her role within her community. One of the enigmatic Three Sisters who appears almost at the end of the work reminds Esperanza of her mission:

> When you leave you must remember to come back for the others. A circle, understand? You will always be Esperanza. You will always be Mango Street. You can't erase what you know. You can't forget who you are. You must remember to come back. For the ones who cannot leave as easily as you. You will remember? She asked as if she was telling me. (105)

At this point, the English meaning of Esperanza's name reveals itself. The name's translation (hope) functions on both a literal and a symbolic level. As a Chicana who rejects the stereotypical roles of submission and victimization, Esperanza represents hope for a different future and the possibility for breaking the cycle of female suffering. At the same time, however, Esperanza does not totally reject her culture or her heritage. Jean Wyatt points out that "viewed from the perspective of the collection as a whole, the stories can be seen as parts of a dialectical process of negotiating with cultural icons that are both inalienable parts of oneself and limitations of one's potential as a woman."[25] Esperanza internalizes the Three Sisters' message and will return, time and again, through her own storytelling and writing, to Mango Street. In so doing, she can eventually become an inspiration for "the ones who cannot leave as easily" (105).

As narrator, Esperanza combines her own story with the stories of the other women on Mango Street. Her storytelling takes on characteristics of a communal narrative in which each component is essential to the other. Esperanza can easily become Marin, Mamacita, Sally, or Rafaela. Her determination to follow a different route, akin to Alicia's goal of attaining an education, prevents her from falling into a recurrent pattern of disenfranchised women. Ironically, the recognition that she is part of this community of women and the realization that she can aspire to something different is only made possible through Esperanza's communal experience with them. The Three Sisters' message, in a way, becomes a metaphor for the artist/writer's responsibility to her community. Even if Esperanza leaves Mango Street behind, the people that she met there and the experiences shared with them will always be part of her memory and part of who she is. It is this memory of past experience that infuses her writing.

For Esperanza, emotional release through writing becomes the unifying force behind her storytelling. In the last section of the work, Cisneros places Esperanza within a circular framework by ending where she begins: telling a story. Yet Esperanza also puts stories "down on paper," (110) which reminds the reader of Aunt Lupe's prophetic words: "You just remember to keep writing, Esperanza. You must keep writing. It will keep you free" (61). Esperanza echoes Aunt Lupe's words in the work's final section and also reveals how seriously she has taken the Three Sisters' advice:

> I write it down and Mango says good-bye sometimes. She does not hold me with both arms. She sets me free. . . . One day I will say good-bye to Mango. I am too strong for her to keep me here forever.

> They [friends and neighbors] will not know that I have gone away to come back. For the ones I left behind. For the ones who cannot out. (110)

Esperanza transcends her social condition through writing, yet what she writes about reinforces her solidarity with her people, especially the women, of Mango Street. In her study on community in ethnic American literature, TuSmith concludes that "while *Mango Street* does not endorse certain culturally sanctioned patterns of behavior—namely, those that are restrictive and abusive to women—its orientation and message are clearly communal."[26] Esperanza can reject stereotypical roles imposed on women by patriarchal structures, yet at the same time, feel solidarity with the women caught in such restrictive roles. That this realization is embodied in a young Chicana's perceptions allows Cisneros, as author, to expose and critique the cultural, social, and economic subordination of confined and abused women through a seemingly naïve, childlike perspective. Yet this conscientious and intentional use of narrative voice does not undermine its literary significance since the power of her critique is significantly latent.

With a collection of vignettes characterized by their poetic and lyrical quality, Cisneros manages to create a distinctive narrative discourse that empowers the female protagonist to define what *she* thinks is best for her instead of what others dictate is her rightful place in society. In this sense, the unconventional structure fits the unorthodox account of a young Chicana's coming-of-age story. The work also captures the dialectic between self/writer and community. Esperanza finds her literary voice through her own cultural awareness and experience with other Latinas. The self-empowerment she seeks through writing coalesces with her commitment to community and with her promise to pass that power on to other women.

While it is true that Esperanza, at times, wants to escape from the confines of Mango Street and yearns for a house of her own, this does not mean that she totally rejects her culture or embraces the "American dream" as critic Juan Rodríguez suggests.[27] What Esperanza wants to leave behind are the culturally inscribed gender roles imposed by patriarchy and manifested through the lives of the women in her neighborhood. What Esperanza longs for is a different "house" in which to nurture her individuality, freedom, identity, and voice. This space also becomes a metaphor for the "house" of storytelling, writing, and artistic/literary creativity. In writing of her reality, she will return again and again to Mango Street since her creativity is nurtured by the communal experience of women's lives. As Caryn Mirriam-Goldberg points out, "eventually both the fictional Esperanza and the real Cisneros find a home in their own hearts. And they make a promise to return and speak for family and friends in the barrio they left behind."[28]

Though *The House on Mango Street* is considered a work of fiction, many readers constantly trace its autobiographical similarities with the author's life. When she first began to write, Cisneros interestingly commented that she "writes about those ghosts inside that haunt me, that will not let me sleep, of that which even memory does not like to mention. . . . Aren't we constantly trying to give up the ghost, to put it to sleep once and for all each time we pick up the pen?"[29] This reference to "ghosts" that haunt her memory and influence her literary creativity is also echoed in the works of other women of color writers such as Maxine Hong Kingston in *The Woman Warrior* and Toni Morrison in *Beloved*.[30] These writers are constantly negotiating the push-and-pull factors of coming to terms with their pasts, with the "haunting" images that surface in their writing, a struggle to address the "unspeakable things unspoken,"[31] and to use this energy as a driving force in their literary representations of gendered and racial experience.

Regarding the conception of her characters, Cisneros also admitted that "what I'm looking for is a kind of generosity with the characters and a heart that understands them, beyond holding grudges or getting revenge. I really believe that when we write there are moments, a few seconds, when . . . the writing transcends us, when we're writing in the light. It's channeled through us so the writing can be wiser, more loving—and then we go back to being ourselves. . . . I think we have to get very humble, and fearless, for the writing to be wiser."[32] Furthermore, Cisneros' statements on how she would like to be understood by the reader offer important insights into her vocation as a writer. In an interview with Gayle Elliott, Cisneros remarks:

> A lot of people mistake the *persona* that I create in my poetry and fiction with *me*. A lot of people claim to know me who don't really know me. They know the work, or they know the persona in the work, and they confuse that with me, the writer. They don't realize that the persona is also a creation and a fabrication, a composite of my friends and myself all pasted together. The real Sandra Cisneros isn't going to be out dancing on tables; she's going to be at a table, writing.[33]

One of the most important rewards that writing *Mango Street* has given Cisneros is the certainty that whether or not her works blur the lines between autobiography and fiction, at the heart of her writing there is an important story to tell and an avid reading audience waiting to receive it. In this sense, Cisneros aligns herself with fellow writers such as Ana Castillo, among others, in trying to fill a void in the literary representation of Chicana experience, an experience that Castillo asserts reveals "women who look and think and feel like me and who have had similar experiences in society. . . . Why should I want to write about characters all too familiar to American literature? They're there already, somebody else has done it. . . . All I can do, in the most convincing and powerful way I know how, is to write from what is true to me."[34]

In 1985, Cisneros won the Before Columbus Foundation American Book Award[35] for the publication of *The House on Mango Street*. Established in 1976 as a non-profit educational and service organization, the foundation honors writers and publishers invested in promoting and disseminating contemporary multicultural literature, thereby demonstrating respect for the wealth of cultural and ethnic diversity that constitutes American writing. The award further consolidated Cisneros' reputation as a talented and praiseworthy author.

Since Cisneros finished and sent the last chapters of her manuscript to her publisher, Nicolás Kanellos, from an island in Greece, she also took advantage of her relocation to explore the region and other European counties. She lived in various countries such as France, Italy, and Yugoslavia. She also relied on her writing talents during these short sojourns in foreign countries. In the spring of 1983, for example, Cisneros served as artist-in-residence at the Michael Karolyi Foundation in Vence, France, where she taught courses on writing and worked on her own poems, which were eventually collected and published by Third Woman Press in 1987 under the title, *My Wicked Wicked Ways*.[36] The artist-in-residence program paid for her living expenses and provided the much-needed space to work on her writing.

For Cisneros, one of the benefits of living and traveling abroad was the interaction with different cultures, languages, settings, and worldviews. She realized the similarities and interconnectedness between people from different parts of the world and how cross-cultural and transnational alliances could be formed, especially among the communities of women she encountered along the way. Cisneros remarks, "I . . . listened to their stories, and I think I made so many friendships that crossed borders. It was like we all came from the same country, the women; we all had the same problems."[37] An example of a lasting and trustworthy friendship forged during these years that has developed over the past two decades is her relationship with Jasna K. While living in Yugoslavia, Cisneros met Jasna in the summer garden they both shared outside their residence. Jasna was a young divorcée who lived in her mother's home; Cisneros was a young poet/writer "playing wife" to her boyfriend Salem, a printer, in charge of the household chores and gardening. The two women met "on the wooden bench outside the summer kitchen of our garden" and felt instantly connected: "you looked at me as if you'd always known me, and I looked at you as if I had always known you, of that we were convinced."[38] They spoke frequently and developed a strong friendship that included sharing their stories and traditional customs with each other. Jasna taught her how to make roasted kaffa (coffee), the Turkish way; Cisneros made a Mexican piñata for Jasna for her birthday.

Their friendship strengthened over the years despite the geographic distance that often separated them. Jasna later visited the United States to work on translating Cisneros' stories into Serbo-Croatian. Ten years after their meeting, during the turbulent wars in Sarajevo between Muslims, Croats, and Serbs, Cisneros would rally whole communities in the United States demanding that governmental authorities help Jasna and those like her captured in the crossfire. After receiving a devastating letter from Jasna describing the horrific conditions in Sarajevo during the war, Cisneros decided to publish the letter in several major newspapers across the country.[39] She then delivered an emotional plea for intervention and empathy with Jasna's suffering: "A woman I know is in there. In that country. . . . That woman, hermana de mi corazón, sister of my heart. I know this woman. And I am in San Antonio, and the days and the hours and the months pass and the newspapers cry: Something must be done! Somebody, someone, help this somebody!"[40] Cisneros gave this moving speech on International Woman's Day in San Antonio, Texas, in support of Jasna's situation. It was also later published in *The New York Times* and other venues. For the duration of the war up to 1996, Cisneros held prayer vigils and meetings, among other activities, to raise awareness of the excruciating circumstances suffered by Jasna's family and countless others in her war-torn country. Such was the extent of Cisneros' commitment to her friendship with Jasna; such is the intensity of her activism for just causes.

Mindful of Cisneros' friendship to Jasna and her commitment in denouncing the atrocities suffered by thousands of men, women, and children, over a decade after the events occurred (2008) a sense of poetic justice arrives with the capture of Radovan Karadzic, one of the masterminds behind the genocide and acts of violence. Despite the fact that he continued to live in Sarajevo under the guise of a white-bearded, alternative medicine specialist, his capture comes as a surprise to those who thought him an invincible fugitive. Yet his detention also confirms that those who promote hate crimes based on prejudice and confrontations sooner or later must deal with the repercussions of their actions through their self-inflicted ignominy. For Cisneros and Jasna, and for the rest of the world that witnessed the news of his capture, Karadzic's arrest and eventual processing for crimes of war signals the healing of an open wound that marked the lives of those who felt its deep laceration and those who sympathized from afar with its affliction.

Cisneros returned to the United States after her initial European travels in 1984, the year that Arte Público Press released *The House on Mango Street*. Though the book was very well received by the reading public, there was still the immediate need to continue supporting herself since the money earned from the publication of her book soon ran out. In 1984 she accepted a position as Arts Administrator for the Guadalupe Cultural Arts Center, which meant that she had to move from Chicago to San Antonio, Texas. The social climate in Texas was quite different from the environment she left behind in Chicago. Suddenly, Cisneros had to come face to face with the distinctions between race, nationality, cultural identity, and the alliances formed or disrupted by these characteristic traits. She explained the contradictions regarding identity formation when she arrived in San Antonio:

In Texas, they are physically closer to the border but emotionally they are far away. We in Chicago are physically farther, but emotionally closer to Mexico. We had relatives in the interior. We had ties to Mexico in a way we did not have ties to Illinois. . . . But in Texas I had to start saying I was Chicana because when I said I was Mexicana they thought I was from Mexico! And I was, kind of. (Laughter) And then I would go to Mexico. If I said I was Mexicana people would look at me. . . . So in Texas I had to start calling myself Chicana even though my family doesn't like it since it moves me one step further away from the country they don't want to loose identity with. My brother always says that "We're Mexicanos." I never deny that I am; I feel very Mexican. But I had to start using Chicano so as not to confuse my audience.[41]

Nevertheless, Cisneros found a very nurturing environment in San Antonio, one that celebrated culture and traditions in ways that resonated with her own need for connection to her Mexican roots. Furthermore, the neighborhood came alive with the sounds of Spanish everywhere she went; she began to thrive in an environment where people knew "how to pronounce your name. Where you can walk down the street and you're not the minority, where 55.6 percent of the population of 935,933 has a Spanish-language surname."[42] In staunch opposition to the places she had previously lived in, San Antonio marked the beginning of a new-found sense of belonging and commitment to a cultural space that not only recognized but also honored her Mexican heritage and her roots. What San Antonio undoubtedly offered Cisneros was a place to nurture her bicultural/bilingual identity, a space in which to celebrate her *Chicanismo* in the midst of her American setting. In her own words, what she describes as:

A landscape that matches the one inside me, one foot in this country, one in that . . . . A place where two languages coexist, two cultures side by side. Not simply on street signs and condominiums. Not simply on menus and bags of corn chips. But in the public and private, sacred and profane, common and extraordinary circumstances of that homeland called the heart."[43]

Cisneros immersed herself in community activities, helping to organize book fairs and art exhibitions that highlighted the talents of the Latino/a community. Yet she was often disappointed with the turnout since very few people outside of the community attended the events. This made Cisneros harbor a growing resentment mainly toward Anglo Americans for showing a lack of interest in the diversity of cultural and artistic expression. She claims that it wasn't until fellow Chicana Norma Alarcón came to visit Cisneros and questioned why she had no Anglo American friends that Cisneros began to realize how much her politics and militancy had influenced her social development and personal relationships. "White people," she stated, "never came into the neighborhood where I worked. I wasn't about to go into their neighborhood and start telling them about Chicano art. I was creating Chicano art and I was bringing Chicano writers to the neighborhood. I was committed to the neighborhood."[44] She also admits that "something ugly happened at that time that I didn't realize. I have to say now that I am in a more balanced place than I was at that period."[45] The schism between Anglo American and Mexican American customs, social spaces, artistic representations, and traditions constantly permeates her worldview, sometimes integrating and connecting seemingly opposing visions, at other times colliding against each other with the same degree of resistance and militancy. Yet Cisneros manages to move forward and to rise above the divisiveness, working to decrease its intensity, while acknowledging its presence.

Cisneros' work at the Guadalupe Cultural Arts Center and her social activism soon left her very little time for writing. Fortunately, in 1985, she received a fellowship from the Dobie Paisano Foundation.[46] Much like the first National Endowment for the Arts fellowship she received that helped her finish *The House on Mango Street*, this new award came at the most appropriate occasion and provided the much-needed space and time for writing that she constantly coveted. The Dobie Paisano Fellowship is sponsored by the University of Texas at Austin and the Texas Institute of Letters. Only Texas residents can apply for the award, which consists of a six-month retreat at the Dobie Paisano ranch, fourteen miles southwest of Austin. The natural beauty and isolated environment of the retreat both inspires and promotes the creative writing process.

Cisneros thrived in the environment of this important retreat. Without having to worry about supporting herself financially, Cisneros concentrated on what came naturally to her through keen, detailed observation. She reveled in the sense of comfort that living in San Antonio provided and for the first time felt as if she had found a home, sometimes "a little sad, a little joyous, that has made me whole."[47] For the remainder of her stay at the Dobie Paisano ranch, Cisneros focused on her poetry, which would later appear in the publication of her first major poetry collection, *My Wicked Wicked Ways*.

For the next two years after the retreat, Cisneros went back to the community of San Antonio where she tried to make a living through public poetry readings and by advertising creative writing workshops. Riding on the success of *Mango Street* and public presentations as well as on visits to schools and universities that assigned her work in classes as required reading, Cisneros became a surreptitiously recognized figure. She remarks, "I'm not famous enough to make an American Express commercial and maybe I'll never be, but I'm the kind of famous that when I go into a local supermarket or shoe store some young child or college student will ask, 'Didn't you visit my class?'"[48] Yet, unable to secure a stable income in the city she considered home, Cisneros was left with few alternatives. In 1987 she accepted an offer to teach creative writing as a visiting lecturer at California State University in Chico. The position offered a steady income and promised a space to continue her own creative writing projects. She reluctantly left San Antonio and headed west.

Soon after her arrival in Chico and her immersion into the university environment, Cisneros realized that the two aspects of her job offer (teaching and creative writing time) were often at odds with one another. The demands of her work schedule, which included preparing for classes, teaching, and grading, often preempted her writing time. She felt torn between dedicating all her energy to helping her students develop their creative writing techniques instead of working on her own material. This balancing act became increasingly difficult, to the point where she asserted that her "private time gets stolen because I can't write. My creativity is going towards them [her students] and to my teaching and to my one-on-one with them."[49] Nor was Cisneros in total agreement with the teaching principles adopted by the institution that strictly abided by prearranged class time schedules and discouraged any further meetings with students outside of class periods. She was often frustrated by the fact that students couldn't benefit from more time to dedicate to their creative writing in class and complained about how her students were cutting their inspiration short in order to attend their next class. These practices, added to Cisneros' notorious reputation for arriving late to class sessions, exacerbated her visiting lectureship, and slowly pushed Cisneros into a troublesome emotional depression. In an interview with Raul Niño she admits: "What happened in 1987 . . . was that I was in a suicidal, depressed period in my life. I was very, very ill then—and very sensitive to any kind of criticism," though she concludes that once she got over that difficult period in her life the writing came "from a very different place," from a stronger, intuitive, mature perspective.[50]

During her year at California State University, Cisneros met up with writer and literary critic Norma Alarcón who would become her lifelong friend and mentor. Alarcón is a specialist in feminist critical theory, cultural criticism, and studies of Chicanas/Latinas and other women of color. Cisneros discovered she had many things in common with Alarcón: cultural background, shared languages, commitment to social activism, similar artistic concerns, and consonant thematic issues in their writing. She quickly realized that neither of them had "the luxury or leisure in our lives for us to write about landscapes and sunsets and tulips in a vase. Instead of writing by inspiration, it seems we write by obsession, of that which is most violently tugging at our psyche."[51] Alarcón helped Cisneros get through the dark period of insecurity and loss of faith in her writing capacities; Alarcón constantly pushed her to move forward despite surrounding circumstances.

Cisneros managed to finish her collection of poems and trusted her friend Alarcón with the work's publication. At the time, Alarcón managed a small press (Third Woman Press) originally founded while she conducted graduate studies in Bloomington, Indiana. In 1987, when Alarcón joined the faculty at the University of California at Berkeley, she brought the press with her. She was actively involved in the press's development and can boast of several commercial successes in its catalogue. What Alarcón originally believed was "an antidote to loneliness," since back in the mid 1980s she felt "there weren't enough other women of color or Latinas in Bloomington for me to have a conversation with,"[52] transformed into an important alternative press dedicated to the publication and dissemination of fiction, criticism, and poetry by women of color. In this sense, Cisneros found the best alternative, literally and ideologically speaking, for the publication of her work.

Two pivotal events in Cisneros' life during the same year as the publication of her first poetry collection would also initiate a significant turn of events for her. The National Endowments for the Arts awarded her a second fellowship, which provided the financial stability to leave the classroom and once again concentrate entirely on her writing. With renewed confidence in her creativity, she initiated contact with Susan Bergholz, a literary agent who had been trying to reach Cisneros for the past three years. Bergholz was interested in helping her publish another work of fiction. Yet Cisneros' convoluted depressive state during her year in Chico, California, had discouraged her from contacting anybody. When she decided to reach out to Bergholz, Cisneros had already been working on several short stories. At the agent's request, Cisneros sent her the stories that she had been working on and within a couple of months Cisneros had a new book contract with a major publisher: Random House/Vintage Press. The contract proved to be a landmark negotiation that won Cisneros a $100,000 advance, the largest sum given to a Chicano/a writer. From this point on, Cisneros was able to rely solely on her writing as a mode of sustenance and as a source of liberating power. With her second NEA grant in hand, Cisneros headed back to San Antonio to continue working on her fiction.

Unlike her first experience while writing *The House on Mango Street,* Cisneros concentrated meticulously this time on meeting the publisher's deadline. She insisted on quality time alone with herself as the only requirement for the creative writing process, which often took up to twelve hours a day. This meant, as she has constantly claimed, that she had to be neither wife nor mother, only having to look after herself: "I come first, and my writing comes first, regardless of anybody in my life."[53] She later concluded: "I really like my solitude. I don't like being lonely, but I'm not lonely. I need to be alone to work. I have very close friends and very close men in my life, but I don't want them in my house. That's the difference."[54] This also meant confronting the skeptical criticism of her family members whose interest primarily focused on her announcing an engagement and impending wedding date. For her relatives, "to be alone, to be exiled from the family is so anti-Mexican. My family still finds my behavior kind of strange. I'm pulled to be with them, and yet to be with them requires an inordinate amount of time."[55]

Cisneros, on the other hand, kept refusing to follow the dictates of a patriarchal world. "There's a lot of stuff going on with women," she states, ". . . as far as figuring out you don't have to go the route that society puts on you. Men are already in a privileged position. They don't have to fight against patriarchy;

it put them in a great place. But the women did; it took us a little while to figure out, 'I don't have to get married just yet,' or 'Wait a second, I don't have to have a baby now.'"[56]

Many of Cisneros' concerns over prescribed gender roles and cultural practices lie at the center of her collection, *Woman Hollering Creek and Other Stories*.[57] Divided into three parts that include twenty-two stories ranging in length from short vignettes to those more stylistically crafted, this collection demonstrates the development of Cisneros' fiction and the broadened scope of her thematic concerns. It offers, as Harryette Mullen explains, the "stories of a variety of women trying various means of escape, through resistance to traditional female socialization, through sexual and economic independence, self-fashioning, and feminist activism, as well as through fantasy, prayer, magic, and art."[58] The collection also displays Cisneros' efforts to reconceptualize traditional images of women, particularly those related to Mexican culture, and to create characters who reflect and embody a *new mestiza consciousness* (following Gloria Anzaldúa's concept) with more specificity and contemporary relevance.

The first part of *Woman Hollering Creek*, entitled "My Lucy Friend Who Smells Like Corn," follows in the vein of the adolescent narrative voice found in *The House on Mango Street*. The first two stories in this new collection, in fact, can be seen as a spin off to Esperanza Cordero's experience in *Mango Street* with her childhood friends, Lucy and Rachel ("Our Good Day," "Laughter," "Born Bad," "Hips," "The Three Sisters," among others). Similar parallels are also evident in the exhaustion of caring for the family after her mother dies seen in stories such as "Sally," as well as the humiliation experienced in the neighborhood and at school due to extreme poverty ("A Rice Sandwich"). In *Woman Hollering Creek*, "Salvador Late or Early" also follows the concern over a child burdened with adult responsibilities. "Mexican Movies" pays tribute to the legacy and influence of Mexican films and the experience of one of the few family outings (a trip to the movie theater) while "Barbie Q" confronts notions of poverty and female beauty through the acquisition of damaged Barbie dolls and the covering up of physical imperfections that do not meet the standards of traditional concepts of beauty. The last two stories in this section, "Mericans" and "Tepeyac," both set in Mexico, deal with cultural identity, border crossings, religious fervor (or its absence), and the power of memory to re-create the past. All of these thematic concerns originally surfaced in *The House on Mango Street*.

Part II, on the other hand, moves beyond a childlike perspective and naiveté to incorporate the experience of a young adult narrator caught in a maturation process constantly threatened by impending danger. "One Holy Night," describes the sexual encounter of an eighth grade girl with a thirty-seven-year-old man who claims direct descent from Mayan ancestors. Chaq Uxmal Paloquín, also known as Boy Baby, lures the narrator into having sexual relations by showering her with gifts, attentions, and what she considers eloquent words describing a glorious past that immediately impress her. From this one encounter, the young girl becomes pregnant much to the chagrin of her strict grandmother/guardian. She also becomes the talk of the town, a shame to the family. Meanwhile, Boy Baby flees from town. His picture later appears in the newspaper, arrested and linked to the murder of eleven girls in the last seven years. Though the narrator equates what she feels for Boy Baby with true love, she never internalizes how close to death she really came. She is still hopeful and looking forward to a future with five children. Yet the experience leaves a lasting impression on her and a sense of disillusionment when she describes her sexual encounter as "a bad joke" to her curious girl cousins, warning them that "when you find out, you'll be sorry."[59] It is through the contextualized message of the story that the reader discerns the precarious conditions, violence, and social stigmatization that lurk in the narrator's life experience.

"My Tocaya" also explores the disappearance of a young girl. Using a conversational tone filtered through interior monologue, the narrator, Patricia Chavez, focuses on the story of a girl who shares her same name but leads a different lifestyle. Patricia Bernadette Benavídez, destined to work in her family's taco business, decides to leave home only to be presumably showcased on the evening news and in all the newspapers as missing, and later identified as the dead body in a ditch. Yet three days after the funeral services she appears in a local police station clarifying the mistake. The narrator's sarcastic criticism over the incidents involving Patricia Bernadette Benavídez is contained in ironic passages involving feelings of disdain and indifference, yet also anger over her notoriety: "When the TV cameras arrive at our school, there go all them drama hot shits howling real tears, even the ones that didn't know her. Sick. Well, I couldn't help but feel sorry for the dip once she's dead, right?" (40). The sarcastic tone, however, glosses over the fact that while Patricia (the narrator) complains about the erratic behavior of her *tocaya,* the body of a murdered girl seems to slip through the story unnoticed. Cisneros' veiled critique here, similar to the one found in "One Holy Night," reveals the life-threatening social conditions of some inner-city neighborhoods to which women are particularly susceptible.

Part III in *Woman Hollering Creek,* subtitled "There Was a Man, There Was a Woman," contains a group of stories more stylistically developed and aesthetically crafted. The stories also focus on the experience of more mature women confronting notions of cultural identity and socialization processes as well as issues regarding race, class, and gender. The section begins with the title story, "Woman Hollering Creek," one of the most frequently anthologized, and ends with a two-part sequel, "Tin Tan Tan" and "Bien Pretty." One of the most memorable stories, "Eyes of Zapata," displays the figure of the revolutionary Mexican hero, Emiliano Zapata, seen through the eyes of his mistress, Inés; an emotionally charged and intriguing narration that combines verifiable historical details with fictional re-creation of events and elements of the spirit world. Another story, "Little Miracle, Kept Promises," takes on epistolary form, collecting short written petitions or peace offerings to various saints, religious deities, and virgins for miracles performed.

Most of the stories in Part III display a unifying thematic concern: claiming and celebrating Chicanas' strength and tenacity in the midst of violence, continuous acts of male chauvinism, and the scrutiny of a society intent on perpetuating traditional gender roles. In "Woman Hollering Creek," the protagonist, Cleófilas Enriqueta de León Hernández, a Mexican bride taken across the border to live what she believes will be a fairy tale marriage, quickly realizes that her idolized husband is a violent domestic abuser who controls her every movement. Pregnant with her second child, she visits a clinic and eventually accepts the help of Graciela and Felice who convince her to escape her abusive relationship. Felice, a woman unlike any other she had seen before, amazed Cleófilas: "The fact that she drove a pickup. A pickup, mind you, but when Cleófilas asked if it was her husband's, she said she didn't have a husband. The pickup was hers. She herself had chosen it. She herself was paying for it" (55). Yet what most astonished Cleófilas was when Felice "opened her mouth and let out a yell as loud as any mariachi" (55) when they crossed the *arroyo* called Woman Hollering Creek, an image associated to the legendary figure of *La Llorona,* the weeping woman of Mexican folklore.

Many versions of the figure of *La Llorona* exist.[60] The most common describe her as a ghostlike, ethereal figure of a woman usually seen around bodies of water. Legend has it that she once drowned her children to run away with her lover and was subsequently punished by God to roam the earth in search of them. Her image is an ill omen of death, but is primarily seen as a symbol of uncontrolled female sexuality and betrayal. Not only does Felice transform the myth of *La Llorona,* but also reconstructs the image into an assertive, powerfully vocal figure in control of her life. When Felice hollers "like Tarzan" (56) as she crosses over the creek and laughs at her own revisionist intentions, she in turn empowers Cleófilas with a new form of being, of relating to the world, and of her place within it. As Virginia Brackett points out, Felice's "triumphant, Tarzan-like shout symbolically replaces the helpless cries of grief that Mexico's traditional mythical women emit. Cisneros does not preach to her readers, but offers a glimpse into Mexican culture and mythology that might spark curious readers to learn more about Mexican ways."[61] By the end of the story, as a result of Cleófilas' interaction with Felice, it is Cleófilas who is laughing, "a gurgling out of her own throat. A long ribbon of laughter, like water" (56), as she moves farther away from male entrapment, abuse, and control.

"Never Marry a Mexican" revisits the themes of cultural identity and racism prevalent in Cisneros' fiction. The narrator, Clemencia, intent on following her mother's advice not to marry a Mexican man due to his chauvinistic behavior, establishes a relationship with her married Anglo American art professor, Drew, and believes she controls her sexuality and sense of independence.

Inadvertently, however, she succumbs to her own passions. She constantly asserts, "I'll never marry. Not any man. I've known men too intimately. I've witnessed their infidelities. . . . I've been accomplice, committed premeditated crimes. I'm guilty of having caused deliberate pain to other women. I'm vindictive and cruel, and I'm capable of anything" (68).

The title of the story, then, brings forth a two-fold manifestation of racism involving the main characters. There is a type of internalized racism operating between the mother's Mexican American side of the family and the father's Mexican-born side of the family, which in several instances resembles Cisneros' descriptions of her own family situation. In the story, the father's side of the family looks down on the wayward behavior of the mother's relatives since they stray away from traditional Mexican customs and are more assimilated to Anglo American ways. There is also a class issue involved, a clash between the working-class environment of the mother's home that welcomes strangers to their kitchen table versus the formality of the father's relatives using tablecloths, fine dinnerware, and napkins while stressing dinner etiquette. So when the mother advises Clemencia not to marry a Mexican, she does so from the perspective of class difference in addition to her disdain for Mexican men's chauvinistic behavior.

In an interesting twist, however, the title also relates to Clemencia and her relationship to her lover, Drew. When he decides to end their affair and continue living with his Anglo American wife, Clemencia reasons: "We had agreed. All for the best. Surely I could see that, couldn't I? . . . Hadn't I understood . . . responsibilities. Besides, he could *never* marry *me*. You didn't think . . . ? *Never marry a Mexican. Never marry a Mexican* . . . No, of course not. I see. I see." (80). While Drew claims to adore her dark skin, indigenous traits, and exotic looks, the relationship never moves beyond a tokenization of her identity, an intimacy with "the other" who can never be seriously considered as an equal in racial standing, as someone to consider as a life partner. In an act of revenge and control, Clemencia decides to seduce Drew's son in the same way she was once seduced by the father. She can even disassociate herself, racially speaking, from hurting Megan, Drew's wife, as she asserts, "If she was a brown woman like me, I might've had a harder time living with myself, but since she's not, I don't care. . . . She's not *my* sister" (76).

Clemencia fails to realize, however, that what she views as a way of getting back at her former lover for his betrayal, is essentially an objectification of her own subject position. At the end of the story, Clemencia remarks, "Human beings pass me on the street, and I want to reach out and strum them as if they were guitars. Sometimes all humanity strikes me as lovely. I just want to reach out and stroke someone, and say There, there, it's all right. There, there, there" (83). Clemencia's upbringing and her socialization process prevent her from establishing real connection or genuine intimacy with anyone. Yet at the same time, she refuses to follow the role models traditionally set out for her (marriage and motherhood) and instead turns to art as her only sustaining life force, a space where neither race nor class dominate, only spontaneity and creativity.

A different relationship comes forth in the two last stories of Part III, "Tin Tan Tan" and "Bien Pretty." The first story is based on an acronym (Lupita), each paragraph beginning with the letter of her name. It is written by Rogelio Velasco (a pseudonym for Flavio Munguía), owner of an exterminating company, to his lover Guadalupe Arredondo. Yet the reader does not know this information until reading the second story, "Bien Pretty," where the narrator, Lupe Arredondo, fills in the background information. "Tin Tan Tan," then, is a poem of sorts, a pouring out of a lover's soul to the one who just rejected him, an overly dramatic plea to win over her love again, in the vein of the best Mexican *boleros,* filled with clichéd phrases transported from one language (Spanish) to another (English).

"Bien Pretty" sets the record straight. Instead of a romantic poet (Rogelio Velasco) there is just Flavio Munguía (owner of La Cucaracha Apachurrada Pest Control). Instead of the ideal model for Prince Popocatépetl, "with that face of a sleeping Olmec, the heavy Oriental eyes, the thick lips and wide nose, that profile carved from onyx" (144), Flavio turns out to have two other wives and seven children in Mexico while also courting Lupe. After his abrupt departure, Lupe goes through a period of frustrated loss, mourning, and spiritual cleansing that also involves burning all of Flavio's letter, poems, photos, and cards, and each and every sketch she ever painted of him. Instead of drowning in her misery over Flavio's abandonment, Lupe decides to reconsider the painting of Prince Popocatépetl and Princess Ixtaccíhuatl that she had been working on and invert the traditional image: "Went back to the two volcano painting. Got a good idea and redid the whole thing. Prince Popo and Princess Ixta trade places. After all, who's to say the sleeping mountain isn't the prince, and the voyeur the princess, right? So I've done it my way" (163). By reconceptualizing the image, Lupe empowers the female figure in the painting to better reflect the lived experience of Chicanas. She lashes out at the stereotypical portrayals of women, especially those displayed in Mexican *telenovelas:*

> I'm watching telenovelas, avoiding board meetings, rushing home from work. . . .
> I started dreaming of these Rosas and Briandas and Luceros. And in my dreams
> I'm slapping the heroine to her senses, because I want them to be women who
> make things happen, not women who things happen to. Not loves that are *tor-*
> *mentosos.* Not men powerful and passionate versus women either volatile and evil,
> or sweet and resigned. But women. Real women. The ones I've loved all my life.
> *If you don't like it lárgate, honey.* Those women. The ones I've known everywhere
> except on TV, in books and magazines. *Las girlfriends. Las comadres.* Our Mamas
> and *tías.* Passionate *and* powerful, tender and volatile, brave. And, above all,
> fierce. (161)

Lupe, unlike Clemencia in *Never Marry a Mexican,* gets over Flavio by moving on with her life and by repositioning herself as conqueror instead of conquered. In this sense, Lupe's character reflects Cisneros' personal belief that the traditional Mexican female role is a myth when Cisneros asserts that "the traditional Mexican woman is a fierce woman. There's a lot of victimization but we are also fierce. We are very fierce. Our mothers had been fierce . . . and very strong. I really do believe that."[62]

"Little Miracles, Kept Promises" also presents a fierce and bold woman who defines her reality and defends her convictions. The story displays an array of petitions and thanksgivings from different writers to both religious and secular figures. These messages are placed around a statue of the Virgin of Guadalupe in what is presumably a Catholic Church altar. The notes vary from petitions for clothes, furniture, shoes, and dishes, to a boyfriend "who isn't a pain in the nalgas" (117); they also include petitions for finding a job "with good pay, benefits, and retirement plan" (118), winning the lottery, getting backpay owed to them, curing a face full of acne, and passing a British Restoration Literature class, among others. Other messages give thanks for surviving a car accident, a cancerous tumor; for making it to graduation and for the birth of a healthy child. One message, written in encoded numerical script, disguises a homoerotic petition from a young man to the Miraculous Black Christ of Esquípulas to watch over his lover, a soldier away at war.

Yet the longest and most descriptive message comes at the end of the story, written by a young Chicana, Rosario (Chayo) de Leon, from Austin, Texas. Chayo has cut off her long braid as a peace offering to the Virgin of Guadalupe for granting her the vision of a multifaceted female figure that merged indigenous, Spanish, and Mexican traditions. When Chayo stops rejecting the submissiveness inherent in the figure of the Virgin and instead understands the power of her ancestors' patience, endurance, and self-sacrifice; when she realizes that the Guadalupana is "no longer Mary the mild, but our mother Tonantzín. . . . When I could see you in all your facets . . . I could love you and finally learn to love me" (128). Chayo's understanding of the Virgin as a true *mestiza* allows her to come to terms with her own cultural identity and history. The symbolic cutting of her long braid represents a rebirth, "my head as light as if I'd raised it from water" (125), in which Chayo can now assume her true bearing, that of a bicultural woman following her own dictates, honoring the women who came before her and learning from their strength, while at the same time carving her own independent path.

The portrayal of the lives of imperfect, struggling, yet strong-willed women in the characters of Cisneros' stories plays against traditional myths and stereotypes by suggesting that women can no longer be placed within the confines of extremist female roles (saints, martyrs, traitors, deserters). Altruistic sentiments and nurturing instincts quickly vanish in the face of domestic violence and tyranny. Images of women seen in popular telenovelas (the jilted yet suffering lover, the sacrificial mother, the abnegated wife) came under strong scrutiny in the artistic hands of Sandra Cisneros. Though she may have included characters personifying these images, her main goal was to intrinsically acknowledge their existence, but at the same time provide alternatives to the cycles of abuse and suffering that these characters exemplified. Whether it was through sheer force of will, communal alliances with other women, educational advancement, or recognition of female empowerment, Cisneros' message emphasizes change, evolution, and an embracing of new paradigms.

Cisneros' work also reiterates that neither is women's place necessarily restricted to the home. In this sense, she participates in what Erlinda González-Berry calls a "rebellion against the forces of oppression" since, at the end of the story, Chayo appropriates "the cardinal icon in whose name so many women have borne the Law of the Father" and transforms it into "the image and likeness of themselves: New Chicanas . . . who have learned that their strength comes precisely from being the daughters of the brown faced virgin [Virgin of Guadalupe] and of their brown faced mothers whose power comes from knowing how to love."[63]

The reconsideration of these images of women is further enhanced by Cisneros' use of vernacular speech and idiomatic expressions, in English as well as in Spanish, and the incorporation of popular *dichos* from Mexican culture in her stories. The combination of these two factors (thematic and linguistic) allows her to integrate the past with the present, the real with the supernatural, the comic with the horrific. In fact, special attention paid to the nuances and the interconnectedness of languages begins with the work's dedication: "For my mama . . . who gave me the fierce language. *Y para mi papa . . . quien me dió el lenguaje de la ternura.*" The traditional method of narrating ethnic experience only through the use of standard English would never have worked as well. Harryette Mullen comments on the linguistic elements of the text when she states:

> That Spanish operates both as an insider code comprehensible to some but not to others, and also as a repressed language in its subordination to English as the dominant language in the U.S., might be read as the primary signification of the entire text of *Woman Hollering Creek*. . . . The untranslatability of the beauty of Spanish, the unpronounceability of Spanish and Amerindian names on the gringo tongue, and the invisibility or discursive silencing of Chicanos are all figured in Cisneros' text."[64]

One of the examples in which the merging of languages sustains the narration of events appears in the portrayal of the transvestite character, Rudy Cantú/Tristán, who taunts death in his dance with la Flaquita in "Remember the Alamo." Tristán performs for avid crowds, which may include a whole floor of relatives from Mexico who "drive all the way from the Valley for the opening show" (65) at the Travisty, situated behind the monumental historical landmark of El Alamo. Tristán metaphorically dares death (in the figure of a woman) to "[s]ay you want me. You want me. *Te quiero.* Look at me. . . . My treasure. My precious. *Mi pedacito de alma desnuda.* You want me so bad it hurts. A tug-of-war, a tease and stroke. Smoke in the mouth. *Hasta la muerte*. Ha!" (65). The emotionally charged scenes of this story simultaneously expose the trials and tribulations of AIDS victims while at the same time acknowledge the victims by listing their names. In Tristán's bilingual consciousness and through his performance, he acquires a degree of connection to a public that adores him and a temporary means of escape from the effects of his disease.

Another example of linguistic merging comes up in "Eyes of Zapata." Cisneros immortalizes the Mexican revolutionary leader Emiliano Zapata's lover and common-law wife by fictionalizing revealing episodes in their life together from her perspective and gaze. In the story, during one of his furtive stays in his lover's (Inés Alfaro) house, she contemplates Emiliano in his sleep and reminisces on their past: "You used to be *tan chistoso. Muy bonachón, muy bromista.* Joking and singing off key when you had your little drinks. *Tres vicios tengo y los tengo muy arraigados; de ser borracho, jugador, y enamorado . . .* Ay, my life, remember? Always *muy enamorado*, no?" (89). Inés' first-person narration continuously relies on Spanish and also on Amerindian words (tlacolol, petate, huipil, yoloxochitl, nagual, huitlacoche, etc.) to authenticate her experience with Zapata, an experience that Cisneros herself laments is scarcely referred to (like that of many other women during the Mexican Revolution) in historical accounts and documents.

Both "Remember the Alamo" and "Eyes of Zapata," as well as other stories within this text, support Reed Way Dasenbrock's argument that "the work a reader does when encountering a different mode of expression can be a crucial part of a book's meaning, since the book may have been designed to make the reader do that work." [65] He concludes that "a full or even adequate understanding of another culture is never to be gained by translating it entirely into one's own terms. It is different and that difference must be respected."[66] Much of Cisneros' writing, in fact, confronts our preconceived notions of race, class, gender, and cultural identity by challenging her readers, on both linguistic and thematic levels, "to broaden his or her horizon of understanding . . . about a work's locus of meaning and value."[67] Cisneros has repeatedly commented: "I am very conscious when I'm writing about opening doors for people who don't know the culture," but she also states "I'm not going to make concessions to the non-Spanish speaker." Instead, she "will try to weave it [Spanish terminology] in the rest of the story so they don't lose it."[68]

This strategy has proved to be a successful trademark of Cisneros' writing. The sensitive treatment and specific attention paid to the mixing of languages; the portrayal of different aspects and particular situations of the women in the stories; the demystification of traditional female myths/legends; and the ironic commentary on behalf of the opinionated narrators enhance Cisneros' collection of stories as an innovative, inspiring, and constructive work of art.

After the publication of *Woman Hollering Creek* in 1991, Cisneros won the prestigious Lannan Literary Award for Fiction.[69] Established in 1987, the

Lannan Foundation provides awards and fellowships/grants to recognize and support writers whose works challenge our understanding of the world, of cultural diversity, of creative freedom while promoting appreciation for the arts. The Foundation promotes the work of exceptional contemporary artists and writers through individual annual awards such as the one Cisneros received in 1991 for $50,000 or through fellowships that provide continued support and time for artists to complete specific projects. Cisneros also won the Anisfield-Wolf Award in 1993 designated specifically to recognize works addressing issues of racism and diversity.[70] This award likewise recognizes books that have made important contributions to our understanding of racism and our appreciation of the rich diversity of human cultures. Winners of this prestigious award have presented the extraordinary art and culture of peoples around the world, explored human rights violations, exposed the effects of racism on children, reflected on growing up biracial, and illuminated the dignity of people as they search for justice.

That Cisneros received both the Lannan and the Anisfield-Wolf Awards for her writing further solidified her artistic achievements by recognizing her creativity and her desire to continue filling a literary void in the representation of Latino/a experience. With the stories in *Woman Hollering Creek*, Cisneros asserts that she wanted to "chart those barrio ditches and borderland arroyos that have not appeared in most copies of the American literary map but which, nonetheless, also flower into the 'mainstream.'"[71]

In addition to the Lannan and her subsequent Anisfield-Wolf Awards, 1991 proved to be an important year for Cisneros in terms of future contracts. Turtle Bay Books offered her a $100,000 advance for another collection of poetry, which she was currently working on and eventually published under the title *Loose Woman*. Turtle Bay Books issued a new edition of *My Wicked Wicked Ways* since the original publisher, Third Woman Press, was no longer publishing. Vintage Press, a division of Random House, reissued *The House on Mango Street* with a 15,000-copy reprint, propelling Cisneros into a book-signing tour through ten cities and providing larger national exposure of her work. Random House also released a Spanish translation of the work by renowned Mexican writer Elena Poniatowska and a spin off of one of the chapters in the work tilted *Pelitos/Hairs* with beautiful illustrations by Terry Ybáñez for grade-school children that pictorially captured the multicultural appreciation of hair textures. A year later, in 1992, *The House on Mango Street* was adapted into a play by Chameleon Productions. A more recent adaptation of the play by Amy Ludwig was performed in 2005 by the East Los Angeles Repertory Theater Company and directed by Jesus Reyes. According to Micheal Sedano, Ludwig "honored the narrative structure of Cisneros' novel" by giving the script "vivid liveliness, filling the large stage with activity and some inspired staging in the acto tradition of teatro chicano."[72]

Linking Cisneros' work to the tradition of *Teatro Campesino*[73] has particular significance since the appraisal aligns her work with Luis Valdez (the founder of the theater troupe in 1965) and with his particular vision of creating performances that addressed the Chicano experience in meaningful ways for all Americans. Just as Valdez challenges the parameters of performance,[74] Cisneros' writing also defies fictional categorizations by merging poetry with narrative, English with Spanish, humor with sadness or pain, tradition with modernity, and ethnographic detail with popular culture. In so doing, Sandra Cisneros creates dynamic storylines that reveal character development, question binary oppositions, and encourage reading from a decentered framework that promotes changes in the ways we view history, society, culture, gender, and traditions.

THREE

"Entering into the Serpent": A Provocative Chicana Poetics[1]

Some of us keep coming back. Some of us love, and some of us hate, some of us both love and hate our borderlands. Some of us remember, some of us forget.

—Norma Cantu, *Canicula*

Victor Hernández Cruz once commented that poets are "the antennas of the race" and that those "who ventured off into writing should be in awe of the possibilities inherent in our tradition."[2] As one of the most critically acclaimed diasporic Puerto Rican[3] poets with close affinity to Chicano/a writers, Hernández Cruz's assertion serves as an appropriate point of reference for discussing Sandra Cisneros' poetic craft. As a writer, Hernández Cruz's efforts to "perceive and explain the truth" while upholding a "sensibility of Hispanitude" resonate with Cisneros' own poetic process summed up in the following quote:

Worlds exist simultaneously, flashes of scenarios, linguistic stereo; they conflict, they debate. Spanish and English constantly breaking into each other like ocean waves. Your head scatters with adverbs over the horizon. . . . To get to the essence of things in this society is a monumental task of awareness.[4]

Cisneros' literary career began with poetry and poetry readings in local coffeehouses and schools in and around her native Chicago. Cisneros clearly distinguishes between poetry writing versus fiction when she asserts that: "poetry is the art of telling the truth, and fiction is the art of lying. The scariest thing to me is writing poetry, because you're looking at yourself *desnuda*. You're always looking at the part of you that you don't show anybody. . . . And that center, that terrifying center, is a poem."[5] She also describes her initial experiments with the poetic process as "exercises in sound and usually not image-based or idea-focused. It was as if someone had given me a drum, and I was discovering how many different sounds I can create. . . . Poetry is a music without music, a melody without syllables and syntax. Without this energy, is it truly poetry? Perhaps for others. Not for me."[6]

Claiming to have written poetry all along while simultaneously writing fiction, Cisneros confesses she was trained to be a poet, both in her undergraduate and graduate work at Loyola University and the University of Iowa Writers Workshop. In fact, many of the sketches that form part of her works of fiction initially began as poems. Yet her experience and her interaction with poets and other writers in literary circles left much frustration and anger. In an interview with Ramola D., Cisneros comments:

> I hate poets—they're so egotistical and full of themselves! No, I don't mean that about individual poets. . . . I mean, when there's going to be a gathering, and I have to choose countries, then I choose citizenship with fiction writers, maybe because my prejudice stays with me from Iowa. My impression there was that poetry belonged to the wealthier classes, it was an issue of privilege. . . . If I have to read any more of those dreadful boring obsessed-with-your-navel poems again I'm going to die. When I'm around poets of the working class, however, I'm very much at home.[7]

Coming from a working-class family and neighborhood was precisely the motivational thrust that launched Cisneros' writing and eventually produced her first publication. After graduating from the Writers Workshop in 1978, she returned to Chicago and eventually began to work at the Latino Youth Alternative High School while engaging in public poetry readings. These appearances gave way to a contract with the Chicago Transit Authority, sponsored by the Illinois Arts Council and the Poetry Society of America, in which her poetry would appear in buses and subways throughout the city along with the work of other famous poets. In 1980, Cisneros submitted her manuscript to a small group called Mango Press, founded by Chicana poet Lorna Dee Cervantes and operating in San José, California. Gary Soto called Cisneros after reading this manuscript and both he and Cervantes decided to print 1,000 copies of *Bad Boys*, a collection of seven poems that immediately caught readers' attention with depictions of urban life in the barrio. Since Mango Press is no longer operating and the book is currently out of print, Cisneros decided to include the poems in her subsequent 1987 collection of poetry, *My Wicked Wicked Ways*.

The poems in *Bad Boys* are a selection from the master's thesis she submitted in 1978. Many of the poems originated with memories of her childhood and are often based on factual events. The "boys" that populate these early poems range from adolescents to father figures with poignant roles in young girls' or women's lives. Yet the boys are always displayed through the gaze of the "girl" or presumably the female poetic voice that describes and depicts their behavior. In "Velorio," reference to the boys occurs when the girls (Lucy, Rachel, and the poetic persona) attend a baby's wake, trying to avoid the boys' aggressive gaze. These girls also appear in Cisneros' fiction, particularly in her first work, *The House on Mango Street,* in vignettes such as "Our Good Day," "Laughter," "The Family of Little Feet," "Born Bad," "The Three Sisters," and the frequently anthologized vignette titled "Hips," as well as in her collection of short stories, *Woman Hollering Creek,*[8] particularly in Part I titled "My Lucy Friend Who Smells Like Corn." The boys are perceived from the gendered perspectives of the girl(s) whose world is often limited and circumscribed by their actions. Another poem involving children is "Traficante," which describes the neighborhood doctor's unorthodox medical treatment (banging a medical encyclopedia on the wound) to cure a swollen hand of a young girl. It also brings to the forefront the precarious health conditions and limited accessibility to adequate health care in poor Latino neighborhoods.

Yet there are also older male figures depicted in these poems such as in "South Sangamon," inspired by her reading of one of Carl Sandburg's poems about a wife-beating. The poem describes the drunken behavior of an abusive father who physically assaults his wife, refuses to leave before trying to kick the door down, and eventually throws a rock through the window. The poem displays the child's complicity with the mother when they both huddle together silently, hoping for the husband/father's eventual departure. The poem brings forth the disruptive cycle of repeated domestic abuse ("a long time of this") and the precautions the mother and daughter take (locking the door, refusing to allow him in, quieting the other children) in order to confront this abuse.

"Arturo Burro" depicts a father who instructs his children to lie about a disabled sibling they have hidden at home whereas "Joe" recalls a fifty-four-year-old mama's boy whom the neighbors refer to as "the boogie man" and who eventually dies in an automobile accident. The idea for these particular poems came from an educational seminar for Latinos/as in higher education, which stressed the need for more trained professionals to teach the mentally handicapped in these communities. Cisneros recalls that at this seminar:

> [s]omeone commented that their statistics on the numbers of children mentally-handicapped in the Latino community were probably incorrect, since Latino people are very proud and hide their half-ones. . . . The idea of having a secret brother fascinated me, and understanding the inability of children to keep secrets gave me the seed from which to work.[9]

Yet not all of these early poems are about children or fathers. "The Blue Dress," for example, presents the encounter of a loveless relationship between a man and his pregnant girlfriend. Cisneros claims that the source for this poem came from the experience of her former lover and that what struck her about the story he revealed was how he described the pregnant girlfriend in a blue dress waving goodbye to him. Cisneros aimed to re-create the emotion tied to that moment, a product of memory, in a nonsequential rendition of events that starts with the end and works its way back to the beginning. The images capture the girl's vulnerability as well as the loveless relationship's inevitable end.

Cisneros' poems and her detailed depictions illustrate a myriad of circumstances in relationships within unorthodox family structures confronted by difficult social realities: death, domestic abuse, poverty, abandonment. In many ways, the poems in this volume also hint at the ambiguity inherent in barrio life: while it embodies an image of integrative cultural space, the barrio also reveals an undercurrent of raced, gendered, and classed confinement that often showcases a less than ideal setting, particularly for girls and women. With this first publication, as Ellen McCracken states, Cisneros "begins to represent the diverse ethnic people of her Chicago barrio through the optic of a critical feminist consciousness. This aesthetic strategy functions as a point of departure for much of her subsequent writing."[10]

Several years later, Cisneros expanded this publication into a sixty-poem volume titled *My Wicked Wicked Ways*.[11] Considered her first major collection of poetry, the book was initially published by her mentor and friend, Norma Alarcón, founder of Third Woman Press, in 1987 as a result of Cisneros' allegiance to Alarcón and her interest in small presses. The book was later revised and released by Turtle Bay Books, a division of Random House, in 1992. Many of the poems contained in this volume initially appeared in magazines and journals such as *Revista Chicano-Riqueña, Nuestro, Spoon River Quarterly,* among others. Cisneros was very skeptical at first about sending her material out for publication. At the beginning of her career, fearing publication rejection, she did not send her work to major presses: "I never questioned it, there was this kind of Jim Crow attitude that was so ingrained, you never questioned it. And now there's still a kind of Jim Crow, but it's like we're at the back of the magazine. . . . When you look at U.S. Latinos—we never get the front page coverage."[12] Cisneros also felt that neighborhood poetry readings and publishing in smaller presses was "a way people could find me,"[13] particularly other Latina women.

The poems contained in *Wicked Ways* span a period of nine years, from her early twenties while attending college up to her early thirties, which she describes as her "wanderings in the dessert."[14] The book is a compilation of the poems she wrote in graduate school, some before and during *The House on Mango Street,* and some written afterward during her sojourns in Europe. Cisneros admits, however, that the poems in this volume are part of her "juvenilia," like publishing a high school yearbook, and that she no longer writes like this.[15] Yet her explorations and interrogations into the tumultuous terrain of female sexuality, hybrid identity, and feminist consciousness set the tone for most of the writing in and after this collection. Cisneros comments:

I found it very hard to deal with redefining myself or controlling my own destiny or my own sexuality. I still wrestle with that theme. . . . These are poems in which I write about myself, not a man writing about me. It is my autobiography, my version, my life story as told by me, not according to a male point of view. And that's where I see perhaps the "Wicked Wicked" of the title.[16]

What Cisneros never bargained for was the controversy set forth by the cover of her book even before readers had a chance to open it. The first 1987 edition dawns a black and white photo of Cisneros, sitting crossed-legged in cowboy boots and a black, low-cut dress staring and smiling provocatively at the camera with a cigarette in one hand and a wine glass nearby. Her lips, part of her gold hoop earrings, and the wine glass are tinted red to match the book's title. Several critics, including feminists, objected to what they considered the cover's overtly sexualized image. Cisneros responded by stating that "the cover is of a woman appropriating her own sexuality. In some ways, that's also why it's wicked; the scene is trespassing that boundary by saying: 'I defy you. I'm going to tell my own story.'"[17] She also claims there was a humorous intent in presenting the photo modeled on black and white film stars like Rita Hayworth and the Errol Flynn years of filmmaking. At the same time she criticized reviewers' presumptions and questioned why a feminist couldn't be sexy when "sexyness [sic] . . . is a great feeling of self-empowerment."[18] As long as a woman is in control of her own sexuality, Cisneros sees no objection in the choice of her book's cover art. In this sense, she remains true to her conviction that in order to be an effective writer, "you've got to go beyond censorship . . . you've got to go deeper, to a real subterranean level, to get at that core of truth."[19]

Many of the obstacles that prevent Latinas from reaching this core level, according to Cisneros, relate to the ways in which Latinas are raised, secluded within the realms of Catholicism and an overwhelming silence regarding their own sexuality. For Cisneros, living in a culture of denial with a two-fold message of sexual abstinence for women, on the one hand, and socially sanctioned promiscuity and infidelity for men on the other, she realized that "discovering sex was like discovering writing . . . you had to go beyond the guilt and shame to get to anything good. Like writing, it could take you to deep and subterranean levels [and] find out things about myself I didn't know I knew."[20] In a controversial article for *Ms. Magazine,* Cisneros articulates how she transformed her rebellious rejection of iconoclastic Catholic images (particularly the Virgin of Guadalupe) into sources of inspiration after conducting research in pre-Columbian history:

When I look at *la Virgen de Guadalupe* now, she is not the Lupe of my childhood, no longer the one in my grandparents' house in Tepeyac, nor is she the one of the Roman Catholic Church, the one I bolted the door against in my teens and twenties. Like every women who matters to me, I have had to search for her in the rubbles of history. And I have found her. She is Guadalupe the sex goddess, a goddess who makes me feel good about my sexual power, my sexual energy, who reminds me that I must . . . "[speak] from the vulva . . . speak the most basic, honest truth," and write from my *panocha.*[21]

Several incidents in her life and people she encountered helped her in this transformative realization that has deeply influenced the topics and concerns of her writing: depression and a near suicide in her thirties, the writing of the Buddhist monk Thich Nhat Hanh, her peace vigils, the writing of other Chicanas (particularly Gloria Anzaldúa), a trip back to Tepeyac, drives across Texas with fellow Chicanas (Cherrie Morage, Norma Alarcón, among others), and her research into the history of the church for the stories and poems she was bound to write. So that most days Cisneros feels, as she says, "like the creative/destructive goddess Coatlicue, especially the days I'm writing, capable of fabricating pretty tales with pretty words, as well as doing demolition work with a volley of *palabrotas* if I want to. I am the Coatlicue-Lupe whose square column of a body I see in so many Indian women, in my mother, and in myself each time I [look] in the mirror. . . . What I do know is this: I am obsessed with becoming a woman comfortable in her skin."[22] With this realization comes a slow yet progressive transformation and maturation of her poetic voice or poetic persona, which she continued to develop throughout the collection *Wicked Ways* and particularly honed in later poems.

Wicked Ways is divided into four parts. The first section directly alludes to an inner-city Chicago setting ("1200 South/2100 West") and is mainly a reappearance of the poems in her out-of-print chapbook, *Bad Boys,* with a few new additions. The poems focus on childhood experiences and the ramifications of cultural enclaves populated by Chicano families. The second part, which carries the book's title, contains eleven poems through the lens of a semiautobiographical poetic persona who challenges gendered stereotypes and preconceived expectations and gender roles, especially those regarding patriarchal family structures. For example, in "Six Brothers," the poetic voice merges her own story living in a household full of brothers with the Brothers Grimm fairy tale of the "The Six Swans." Yet in equating her experience with the siblings in the tale, the poet also reconfigures her own position in the family as she disrupts her father's expectations and plans. In the process she claims: "I've got the bad blood in me" and, like the youngest brother in the family, finds it difficult "to keep the good name clean."[23]

Another poem that returns to the trope of the six brothers is "His Story" in which the poet presents the father's perspective and her defiant stance against his advice. The father warns her about the history of ill-reputed women in the family: a great aunt who served as mistress, a prostitute cousin, a great-grandmother who dies mysteriously. He also remarks on the coincidence of foul play linked to her name: *tocayas* (girls with the same name) whose delinquent behavior stems, according to the father, from disobeying patriarchal, socially sanctioned norms that often results in disavowal, curses, and widowhood. The poet also ponders on the unlucky fate of women born into a family of male siblings whereas the father regrets that out of all his children, the only daughter (and not the sons) is the one who decides to leave home. Moreover, in "The Poet Reflects on Her Solitary

State," the poetic voice considers the results of her seemingly disrespectful behavior. Solitude and isolation are the price the poet pays for confronting her father's demands, disrupting his expectations, dismantling gendered stereotypes, and being the first to leave home instead of her brothers. Yet she also transforms this price into positive assets—space, time, energy, and creativity with which to write. Similarly, on a literal level, Cisneros realizes that her need for "a room of her own" may be considered an act of selfishness from a patriarchal cultural standpoint. But she also understands that this is the best way to nurture her creativity and allow her voice to come into its own in written form. In an interview with Hector Torres, Cisneros comments on the struggle of women writers, particularly Latinas, in forging this space:

> I think that we've fought for and succeeded in getting in our spaces, our rooms of our own to write in . . . instead of supporting someone who has a room of their own, or living vicariously through someone else's career. It's taken a lot for us to fight for this space. . . . That realization has allowed us the luxury of indulging in our writing. . . . You waste a lot of energy going through all these emotional tugs-of-war within yourself. It's taken a while for women to realize that the space they have to write is something they can value.[24]

This valuable space has been a powerful resource in the development of Cisneros' writing. Yet it has also brought forth much contention, which, in many ways, feeds into the poetry collection's title. According to Tey Diana Rebolledo, Cisneros' work "illustrates the progression of wickedness, and it acquires added dimensions of freedom and power that include sexuality, but go even beyond it."[25] In other words, as Rebolledo states, "to be wicked, then, is to know that you have sinned—against the church, against your parents, against the norms of society."[26] To leave your home; to shun marriage and motherhood; to lead an independent, self-supporting lifestyle; to control your own sexuality—these are the *wicked ways* that Cisneros perceives she and other women are judged for, and these are the topics that lie at the heart of her literary/thematic concerns.

Several poems in this section also deal with women's relationships, love affairs, and the need to constantly address their sexuality. From the very title poem, the poetic persona knows that she "will turn out bad" (24). In "I the Woman," the poet describes herself as "the notorious one," "a live wildness left behind" (29–30) with the same degree of rebelliousness used in "Love Poem #1" in which she is "rowdy as a drum," "a wicked nun" (34) while craving for unknown erotic adventure in "Something Crazy." Cisneros' poetic persona steps into roles and spaces traditionally relegated to men: the lover, connoisseur, transgressor, bar drinker, the wickedly unreligious. The defiant female body that emerges in these poems confronts the boundaries set forth by fathers, culture, tradition, and by hegemonic ideals of femininity.

The third part of *Wicked Ways* is Cisneros' attempt to free herself and her verse both physically and metaphorically. The poems in this section titled "Other Countries" were mainly written during her travels abroad. The journey, as Adriana Estill points out, "allows for an escape from both the barrio's limits and from the speaker's family's strict gender driven expectations" while at the same time "crystallizes the body of the Chicana speaker in order to give her strength and standing."[27] From 1982 to 1984, Cisneros traveled through several countries in Europe (France, Italy, Spain, Greece, Sarajevo, etc.). The memories of the countries and the experiences she lived along the way eventually resurfaced in the themes and topics of the poems collected in this section.

An important theme throughout these poems is the theme of independence. In "Letter to Ilona from the South of France," the poetic speaker cannot find the words to describe her state of elation over her freedom and determination to roam foreign geographic spaces, especially when she feels she has lived, to a certain extent, a cloistered, fearful, uneventful life. The poet's fascination with her new-found independence overwhelms her as she strives to find the words to describe to her friend what it feels like "to wander darkness like a man" (44). In "Letter to John Franco—Venice" the poetic voice ponders on the possibility of ending an affair precisely because she has the freedom of choice to do so when she asks: "Tell me, / one artist to another, / what does a woman owe a man, / and isn't freedom what you believe in? / Even the freedom to say no?" (50). There is also the image of liberating freedom in "Moon in Hydra" when, after years of living under chauvinist ideologies the women decide to abandon gendered constraints, to be the arbiters of their redemption from patriarchal mores, to break away from the myths that linked them to dependency. Other poems scrutinize the role of women in relationships. "Ladies, South of France—Vence" presents a promenade of wives strolling with their husbands in the same park alongside single women who "gather like dusty birds beneath their paisley and polka dot . . . parasols" (45). Yet far from showcasing the married women as superior or better off, the poem presents the image of the unmarried women as valid an option as those who walk with their husbands; perhaps the single women even more joyous as they sing.

The most intimately revealing poems are the ones in which the poetic speaker engages in flirtatious and sexual affairs with men, often bordering on obsessive and erratic behavior (as in "Beautiful Man—France," "Postcard to the Lace Man—The Old Market, Antibes," "Letter to John Franco—Venice," "To Cesare, Goodbye," "Trieste—Ciao to Italy," "Fishing Calamari by Moon," "One Last Poem for Richard," and "For a Southern Man"). A strong sense of adventure, of risqué behavior, of unapologetic surrender characterizes the writing of these poems. At times there is a certain sadness and nostalgia that permeates the mood of the poetic persona and triggers a symbolic empathy with "the underdogs, . . . the survivors, the ones that get away" (60). Yet the predominant image in these poems is that of a self-assured lover who delights in the pleasures of sexual relations and in the power to willfully disengage from any relationship at any time.

One particular poem in part three presents a confrontation with suicide in "December 24th, Paris—Notre-Dame." The images of this poem are particularly haunting since the poetic speaker merges scenes from a rainy day along the Seine River with the prospect of death embodied in a female corpse. Yet the possibility of finding this body evaporates before it materializes in the last stanza of the poem with her allusions to rebirth, vibrant energy, and a strong desire to live: "A year ends/ merrily. Merrily/ another one begins./ I go out into the streets once more./ The wrists so full of living./ The heart begging once again" (46). Poems such as this one and others in "Other Countries" illustrate Cisneros' movement away from the topics and concerns of her earlier poems (in *Bad Boys*), which primarily focused on life in the barrio. The poems in this collection reveal a more eclectic and keen observation of life as she inhabits different geographic and social spaces. The common thread that unites these poems, however, is a feminist consciousness and maturation process that develop as a result of her exposure to different settings and cultures and as she forges intricate relationships with people in different parts of the world.

The fourth and final section in *Wicked Ways* titled "The Rodrigo Poems" is a combination of poems that also engage a feminist perspective in an attempt to negotiate personal relationships and address the themes of love and deceit. The poems are physically descriptive and border on the erotic. Topics include infidelity ("A Woman Cutting Celery"), divergent views of love ("Valparaiso," "I Understand it as a Kiss"), divorce ("No Mercy"), love affairs ("For All Tuesday Travelers," "Beatrice," "The So-and-So's," "Amé, Amo, Amaré," "New Year's Eve"), and also tormented love and abandonment ("Rodrigo de Barro," "Rodrigo in the Dark," "Monsieur Mon Ami," "Drought," "14 de Julio").

Two poems, however, operate on a different level and ultimately reveal a more cosmopolitan and worldly voice. The poem "By Way of Explanation" presents a rebellious and multicultural poetic speaker through depictions of her body linked to different countries or sites (Madagascar, the Amazons, Egypt, Morocco, Andalusia, Tierra de Fuego, Quintana Roo, among others). As Adriana Estill points out, "the speaker of 'By Way' defies simple answers to questions of national identity, political alliance, and origin as she spreads her body through space and resists easy classification."[28] The poem also epitomizes resistance, strength, and assertiveness through the different histories of the particular geographic spaces she embodies in her biographical map. Hers is a story of contention and plurality. Similarly, the final poem of the collection presents a tangential linguistic dimension that relates to her multidimensional world order when the speaking subject resorts to Spanish. "Tantas Cosas Asustan, Tantas" was written during the time that Cisneros was living in San Cristobal de las Casas in Chiapas, Mexico, with her friend, Norma Alarcón. Cisneros admits that she doesn't usually write in Spanish because she lacks the same "palette" that she has in English though Spanish is the language that she relies on when she travels to Mexico. Yet she also remarks that at the time of writing this poem she was "thinking and dreaming in Spanish, and the poem came out in Spanish. When I tried to translate it into English, it sounded wrong to me and I had to leave it in Spanish."[29] Waking up from a nightmare she repeated the words: *tantas cosas asustan* (so many things frighten), and this became the poem's subject matter. Among the things that frighten her she mentions the dead and the living, darkness, silence, the infinite and the finite, love, the moon, and generals. The theme of independence is also woven into the images of this poem when she questions the value of being alone versus perpetually being with someone: "¿Cuál es peor? / Estar siempre sola, / o estar con alguien para siempre" (102). The poem ends with a diametrically opposed image to the title. Happiness ("la felicidad"), on the other hand, never frightens, "tiene que ver con papalotes" (103). Kites (papalotes), a recurrent motif in Cisneros' writing, signal the blissful sense of elation and absolute ease with which she confronts the many things she recognizes as frightening, and serve as a dominant symbol for her strong, independent spirit.

The reedition of *Wicked Ways*, published by Turtle Bay Books, contains a four-page preface poem written on June 11, 1992, in Hydra, Greece. In it, Cisneros introduces the collection of poetry as a representation of her "girl grief decade" (ix). She laments not having role models to follow, and admits that her felony was her desire ("an absurd vice") to be a writer in a traditional patriarchal family where marriage and motherhood were the most viable and socially sanctioned options for women. And though she suffered the effects of solitude and family estrangement for chucking the life her father had planned for her, she also admits that she benefitted from going against the grain and actually enjoyed the myriad experiences of living by her own dictates instead of those dictated upon her. Finally, she places the poems within a specific spatial and temporal dimension by recognizing the evolution of her literary voice. By the time the 1992 edition was released, Cisneros had moved on to different projects, experiences, and narrative and poetic styles, yet always remained conscious of her role as a writer and her increasing recognition as a major figure both in and out of the Chicano/a literary circuit.

Wicked Ways marked Cisneros' appropriation of a feisty, rebellious, provocative poetic voice that blurred the lines between incidents in her life and her imagination/creativity. Her work also crossed the borders between countries (United States, Mexico, Europe), languages (English, Spanish), and genres (poetic prose, narrative poetry). Though the poems span close to a decade of literary production and are not necessarily representative of the poetic voice she currently utilizes, this ground-breaking work, along with the publication and reeditions of *The House on Mango Street*, helped catapult Cisneros' literary career and solidified her reputation in contemporary literary circles.

Seven years after the publication of *Wicked Ways* and another work of fiction (*Woman Hollering Creek and Other Stories*), Cisneros returned to poetry writing with her collection *Loose Woman*.[30] Putting together the compilation of poems for this volume proved to be an exercise in editorial creation. She refers to them as "poems I threw under the bed, metaphorically, thinking of Emily

Dickinson, poems too dangerous to publish in my lifetime."[31] Cisneros comments on the process by pointing out that:

> the collection was in these different typefaces that kind of documented my poverty and my rise out of it. Some poems were composed on my junky little typewriter—the one that made little holes with the o; there were some on my little typewriter that was a step up, an electronic one; all the way finally to computers. So you could see these different typefaces over the years. . . . I think the success of the book is partly because I wrote it as if it could not be published. It's looser in form. It's loose in every which way you can think of. . . . [32]

The title also originated from this process. They are *"poemas sueltos,"* Cisneros remarks, "because they didn't belong to any other collection. . . . They're loose poems. But they're loose 'women' poems. You see? I'm reinventing the word 'loose.' I really feel that I'm the loose and I've cut free from a lot of things that anchored me."[33] But the title also invokes the sexually transgressive undertone of the phrase in English, which lies at the heart of several important and widely anthologized pieces from this collection.

The poems in *Loose Woman* represent an innovative, experimental phase in Cisneros' poetic creation that involves a freer, colloquial voice and playful attitude toward some of her subject matter. She wanted to "get away from the tethers of the Writers Workshop and to be able to be very irreverent and to write as if I were sitting in the Dunkin' Donuts shop and not at the Iowa Writers Workshop."[34] Nonetheless, the poems still retain the cutting-edge, fierce language and feminist consciousness employed in her other writing. Xochitl Estrada Shuru points out that the poems collected in *Loose Woman*:

> illustrate Cisneros's vision of the multiplicity of physical, emotional, and psychological components that in their totality comprise the female poetic subject. . . . While the representation of a multi-faceted personality may strike some as abnormal, eccentric or mad, Cisneros's poetry attempts to depict the undecipherable woman who resists reductive analyses of her complex identity as the norm of female existence.[35]

Loose Woman is divided into three parts. The first part, "Little Clown, My Heart," consists of eighteen poems ranging in length from two or three stanzas to two or three pages. For the most part, these poems concentrate on Cisneros' appropriation and celebration of a female poetic voice that ponders on a range of issues: love, religion, biculturalism, gender roles, poetry writing, long-distance relationships, among other concerns. The section's title poem ("Little Clown, My Heart") is emblematic of the writing as a whole when it presents the carefree, innocent, and trusting excitement of living; the frenzy and thrill of deep feeling; the inquisitiveness and uncertainty of decision-making; yet at the same time the foolish carelessness of surrender.

Other poems, such as "You bring out the Mexican in Me," play on the litanies of Catholic prayer by repeating images linked to Mexican cultural identity, both religious and secular. The poetic persona addresses her lover and the characteristic traits he brings out in her from their shared relationship. Yet the poem may very well address, as Barbara Hoffert points out, "the act of writing itself, which clearly brings out the best in [Cisneros], along with the passion she associates with her Mexican roots."[36] Most of the images in this poem are strong, obsessive, bordering on the violent side of personal attachment: Mexican spit-fire, Aztec love of war, fierce obsidian, lust goddess without guilt, delicious debauchery, etc. The images present all-consuming passion, "Love the way a Mexican woman loves,"[37] with no regrets or recriminations. McCracken remarks that "the modified ritualistic incantations praise the poet's ethnic self that the lover helps to validate. Instead of the religious supplicant praising the dozens of titles of the Blessed Virgin in asking repeatedly for intercession, the Chicana poet valorizes herself through the aspects of her Mexicanicity that the U.S. melting pot has traditionally undervalued."[38]

Still, other poems bring issues of gender to the forefront. In "Old Maids," the poetic speaker observes the ways in which her relatives look down on the unmarried women in the family and associate their single lives with an emotionally troubled childhood or upbringing. Yet instead of buying into the relatives' view of them as "Old Maids" by Mexican standards at the age of thirty, these women (including the poetic persona) have studied other married women's lives and have remained single out of *choice*. This assertion, in turn, leads to a confrontation with and reconceptualization of social/cultural expectations and preconceived gender roles related to marriage and motherhood. The poem advocates a spouseless alternative for women as a viable option vis-à-vis the increasing number of unhappy, unfulfilled marriages, particularly those of the women in her own family. On the other hand, the poems with overtly sexual imagery are those that represent love affairs and long-distance relationships. In poems such as "Christ You Delight Me," "En Route to My Lover I am Detained By Too Many Cities and Human Frailty," and "Love Poem For a Non-Believer," the unapologetic and irreverent poetic voice pours out her inner most feelings of sexual longing and sensual surrender.

The second part of *Loose Woman* titled "The Heart Rounds up Its Usual Suspects," consists of twenty-one poems more intimately related to incidents of despair, solitude, suicidal instinct, primordial love, rejection, and abandonment. They hover in those unspeakable spaces that inhabit the human heart and startle the reader with a fierce honesty and relentless urgency that overflow with grief, anger, and disillusion. These poems also capture the poignancy of turbulent dependency and detailed sexual imagery as the poetic voice tries to come to terms with her sexuality, sense of loss, and bitter spitefulness. At times the poems present a vengeful and distraught woman lashing out and disrupting her lover's placid life and traditional home as in "Pumpkin Eater" and "After Everything." Other poems focus on solitude and abandonment ("The Heart Rounds Up Its Usual Suspects," "Waiting for a Lover," "I am So Depressed I Feel Like Jumping in the River Behind my House But Won't Because I'm Thirty-Eight and Not Eighteen," "I Want to Be a Father Like the

Men," "Amorcito Corazón," "A Little Grief Like Gouache," and "Full Moon and You're Not Here"). Some of the most anthologized poems are the ones dealing with the art of writing and the negative effects of the poet's pursuit of a writing career such as "Bay Poem From Berkeley," "Night Madness Poem," "Unos Cuantos Piquetitos" (inspired by a 1935 painting by Frida Kahlo with the same title), and "Small Madness." These poems set forth the vulnerability and sincerity with which the poet surrenders her work to the reading public's scrutiny. Cisneros considers, in some instances, that readers and/or literary critics do not recognize the laborious nature of the writing process nor do they appreciate the poem's original intent and purpose. Just like the victimized woman stabbed dozens of times by her lover in Kahlo's painting, so is Cisneros' poetry when she surrenders her writing to the perusal and possible wounding of a reader's or critic's interpretations as she presents "the bull's eye of my heart" in her writing, the "jugular," the "wrists," and the "womb" of *mis palabras* (59).

Interracial relationships also find their way into Cisneros' poetry when she cautions the reader against the dangerous *alacrán güero* (white scorpion as a metaphor for white male) and its destructive force when engaging in *liaisons* with Latinas (an experience Cisneros claims to know well). In "Perras" the poetic voice bemoans the fact that Mexican men "acting white" covet the girlfriends of white men "acting Mexican" and thus doubly betray their relationships with Mexican women. The poems with the most overtly sexual imagery focus on provocative sensual pleasure ("Well, If You Insist"), desire for unbound sexual gratification ("Thing in my Shoe"), and forbidden love ("I Don't Like Being in Love"). The only poem that breaks away from the thematic concerns of the others in this section is the poem she writes to her friend Jasna, "I Awake in the Middle of the Night and Wonder if You've Been Taken." Cisneros' relationship to Jasna began when she lived in Sarajevo and has since grown into a significant and lasting friendship.[39] In the poem, Cisneros writes: "At any moment, a precise second might claim you./ At any decisive point, God might not give a damn./ You're there, in that city. You don't count. You're not history" (64). Cisneros' solidarity with Jasna and the civil war raging in Sarajevo spurred not only her writing but also her social activism as well. Cisneros admitted her sense of helplessness in changing the situation at the time, her fear for her friend's life, and the impotence she felt as she realized their lack of empowerment as women. Yet there is strength in Cisneros' act of artistic solidarity, in dedicating this whole collection of poetry to Jasna ("as if our lives depended on it"). The act of writing Jasna into life became an act of preserving that life against all odds. In Cisneros' words, "what you say, whether it is in print or in front of a microphone . . . can go out and kill or go out and plant seeds for peace."[40] She admits that her acquaintance with Jasna motivated her to speak out when all else seemed to fail:

> The only thing that made me different from everyone else in my neighborhood was that I knew the address of someone in Sarajevo. That's why I had been asked

to speak at the International Woman's Day rally. . . . Making that speech . . . made me realize that I wasn't powerless. I could be very mindful and not forget my friend. I don't have to talk about Jasna all the time as long as I know that everything I do is going to affect her.[41]

The last part of the poetry collection, titled "Heart, My Lovely Hobo," shifts the focus of attention to reveal a much more independent poetic persona, in control of her life, her actions, and her own sexuality. The motif of the heart returns in the title poem of this section, this time less foolish and clownish than the poem that initiates the first part of the poetry collection. Pain and suffering are still latent though transitory. Several poems focus on the act of writing and how poetry replaces personal relationships ("Once Again I Prove the Theory of Relativity," "My Nemesis Arrives After a Long Hiatus," "Vino Tinto"), or at times poetry writing is the most important event in her life, a cherished space for creativity ("A Man in my Bed Like Cracker Crumbs," "Bienvenido Poem for Sophie"). Other poems are dedicated to girlfriends and express solidarity, admiration, companionship, and love ("Black Lace Bra Kind of Woman," "Las Girlfriends," "Champagne Poem for La Josie"). One poem in particular is dedicated to her godson (Arturo Javier Cisneros Zamora) on the occasion of his baptism. In the poem "Arturito the Amazing Baby Olmec Who is Mine by Way of Water," Cisneros celebrates her godson's birth and wishes three things for him in life: nobility, wisdom, and generosity. Though she admits that Arturo was stuck with "the aunt who dislikes kids and Catholics" (98) for a godmother, she boasts of the amazing gifts that godmothers can give, which in this case become the three wishes. Her expectations for this godchild exalt heroic historical figures like Emiliano Zapata and Mahatma Gandhi and merge history, culture, and religion by referring to the figure of Mother Teresa and her generosity, thus providing three positive role models for him to follow in life.

Similar to part two, another poem in this section pays homage to her admiration and respect for the Mexican artist Frida Kahlo. In the first part of "Los Desnudos: A Triptych," the poetic voice replaces the nude woman in one of Francisco de Goya's paintings (The Naked Maja) with one of her lovers and similar anatomic images, shifting the gaze of a male voyeur in the original painting to a female who contemplates her lover with a mischievous sexual appetite. In the second part of the poem the subject shifts to the figure of Zapata as metaphor for her affair with a married man. The last part of the poem presents her inability to forget or let go of her lover, which are, coincidently, the same feelings she projects in her poetry writing.

One of the most controversial poems in this collection, "Down There", is a response, on the one hand, to John Updike's poem "Cunts" and, what Cisneros considers, his inadequate use of poetic imagery related to a quintessentially female experience (menstruation). On the other hand, the poem is also a direct confrontation against her students' compulsion to address crass subject matter. In an interview, Cisneros remarks that, in part, she wrote the poem for two of her male students while teaching at California State University:

> I had two freshmen in an introduction to creative writing class, and I couldn't make them understand. They would write these poems every class period to try to gross each other out. They were in a competition of picking gross subjects. You know, kind of locker room material. . . . My criticism was that these weren't poems. . . . I wrote the poem overnight as a gift to them, to show them what I meant. . . . I try to talk about the things that make me a little uncomfortable. Then I know I'm on the right track.[42]

The poem startles the reader with vivid imagery of the appearance, texture, and odor of menstruation while the poetic voice reappropriates the strength of the images and transforms them into a woman's inkwell as she writes a "poem of womanhood" (84). Regarding these lines, McCracken points out, "in a splendid inversion of men's prerogative to address any subject no matter how off-color, Cisneros' poem represents a woman speaking for herself on subjects she chooses in order to please herself, whether taboo or not. The euphemism 'down there' of the title is belied by the bold, confident speech of the poem itself."[43]

The last poem of the collection is the title poem, "Loose Woman." It is perhaps Cisneros' most audacious attempt to situate women's writing vis-à-vis men's confiscation of the written word by redefining the role of the woman poet whose words can be "diamonds and pearls" or "toads and serpents" (112–113). The poetic speaker does not shrink from the epithets hurled at her (beast, bitch, *macha*, hell on wheels, fire and brimstone, among others); instead she revels in her strength to tame the mobs while she builds her "little house of ill repute" (113). Her tongue-twisting self description is the poem's most revealing trait: "I'm an aim-well . . . sharp-tongued,/ sharp-thinking,/ fast-speaking,/ foot-loose/ . . . let-loose,/ woman-on-the-loose/ loose woman./ Beware, honey" (114–115). Her fearless, shameless, and sassy attitude toward life and toward her detractors help position her as a steadfast, determined woman ready to live her life not vicariously through others, not defined and circumscribed by others, but purposefully on her own terms, akin to Cisneros' own life story.

Though Cisneros admits that when she wrote *Loose Woman* she was "writing from a dangerous fountainhead . . . to get the thorn out of the soul of my heart,"[44] these poems reflect a keen maturation process in her writing that helped her come to terms with controversial issues in her life and provided the necessary distance with which to address them. The collection received less reviews (some of them quite negative and, according to Cisneros, hurtful) than her other works. Yet the collection garnered accolades and praise (seen on the book's Turtle Bay cover jacket) from fellow Latina writers (Cristina García, Julia Alvarez, Ana Castillo, among others) who celebrated Cisneros' writing as "fierce, intoxicating, hilarious . . . poems to shout out loud" and as "sassy, tangy, intimate poems." Ana Castillo's words particularly summarize the work's reception:

> *Loose Woman* is a collection of love poems for the nonbeliever, some sheer jade and some for the jaded, a noose for the lover on the loose, a net for the next *novio*. But sometimes they are simply love poems in wonderment of life and death. At all times, Sandra Cisneros has penned poetry of utterly divine language and imagery.

The level of commitment to and satisfaction in her own creative process makes this poetry collection one of the most important contributions of Cisneros' literary career.

FOUR

Caramelo: Weaving Family and National History into Storytelling

Para poder trascender en la historia y que nuestras hazañas se recuerden, es necesario que alguien mencione nuestro nombre.

—Marilola Pérez, "Lengua: Agentes encubiertos"[1]

The U.S.–Mexico border[2] stretches approximately 1,969 miles and divides four North American states (California, Arizona, New Mexico, and Texas) from six Mexican states (Baja California, Sonora, Chihuahua, Coahuila, Nuevo León, and Tamaulipas). On the U.S. western Pacific coast, its line divides San Diego, California, from Tijuana, Mexico, as it crosses the continent to the Gulf of Mexico and ends between Brownsville, Texas, and Matamoros, Mexico. In the United States, Texas has the longest border connecting both countries and California has the shortest. In Mexico, the shortest border with the United States belongs to Nuevo León, whereas Chihuahua shares the longest territorial connection. Contrary to public perception, construction of the wall or barriers that divide these two countries does not represent one continuous structure but rather a grouping of short physical walls beginning and stopping at various locations. This division also contains "virtual fences" authorized, in part, by the Secure Fence Act of 2006.[3] The fences include a system of sensors monitored by U.S. Border Patrol agents.[4]

Approximately 11.8 million people live along the U.S.–Mexico border area.[5] According to the U.S. Department of State Visas Statistics, in 2005 the United

States issued 906, 622-nonimmigrant visas for Mexicans to enter the U.S. territory. Yet statistics provided by the Pew Hispanic Center estimate that the following year (2006) approximately 6 to 7 million Mexican immigrants entered illegally. Public officials estimate that Border Patrol catches one out of four illegal border crossers. Statistics are also kept of immigrants arrested near the southern border between the two countries, who are designated "Other Than Mexicans" or "OTMs." The number of OTMs taken into custody has increased dramatically from 28,598 in 2000 to 65,814 in 2004. Other estimates indicate that over 155,000 non-Mexican individuals were caught trying to enter the United States along the southwestern border in 2005.[6]

What do these staggering and overwhelming statistical details mean for U.S.–Mexico relations and why has a constant, though precarious and life-threatening, flow of people across the border continued to this day? How are these relations confounded across racial, ethnic, class, and gender lines? Most importantly, how have contemporary authors dealt with the personal and national implications of immigration and settlement patterns in their literary works? The history and complexity of U.S.–Mexico border crossings go beyond the scope of this study, but this brief, generalized discussion serves as a point of reference to engage in the analysis of Sandra Cisneros' lengthiest and most ambitious work to date: her novel *Caramelo or Puro Cuento*. Though Cisneros includes a disclaimer at the beginning of the work indicating that the narration is embellished with her own storytelling techniques, she nonetheless admits that the story is based on her father's life. And her father's story is, in turn, the story of millions of Mexican immigrants who share a common goal: movement *al norte* to the United States from Mexico in order to begin a new life, fulfill the precepts of the American Dream, and provide a different lifestyle for their families, rooted in their Mexican language and traditions.

Published in 2002 by Knopf (a division of Random House) in a simultaneous bilingual launching (with a 150,000-copy print run in English and a 13,000-copy print run in Spanish), the long-awaited and much anticipated novel was well-received by Cisneros' loyal reading public. The title is a Spanish word that remains the same in both language issues. The only distinctive factors between the two versions are the book covers' color schemes and a small banner "en español" on the Spanish edition. Several booksellers placed the Spanish-language version on display alongside the English-language version, a successful marketing strategy that began at Borders Bookstore in Puerto Rico with other Latina writers.[7] Cisneros' book is the first of its kind to be launched simultaneously in both languages.

With *Caramelo*, Cisneros also initiated a twenty-city author tour from the date of its publication in October to early December 2002. The tour began in Cisneros' hometown during the Chicago Book Festival with two readings: the first at the Latino Community Center and the other at the Women and Children First Bookstore. She initially read from the unpublished version of the work on April 10 at the Crystal Cove Auditorium (University of California at Irvine), where she stressed "the emotional connection a writer should have with their subject matter" and created immediate rapport with audience members who were "enraptured—and left wanting to hear more."[8] Subsequent presentations took place in different cities, such as Los Angeles and New York, which included schools, universities, and public libraries, aside from programmed visits to Spain and Mexico.

Cisneros also worked on an unabridged audio version of the novel, which took a week to complete due to the length of the work. The final product consists of sixteen hours of recording licensed by Harper Audio mainly geared toward public library and student audiences as well as Cisneros' loyal followers interested in her work in a different format. Cisneros' incursion into the audio book industry demonstrates her willingness to engage in other forms of disseminating her writing that are more in tune with modern readership and literary audiences. She is also one of the few Latino/a authors to explore this alternate form of artistic representation and to see her work actually prosper in the realm of the audio books industry. Though she admits that she couldn't convey each and every character's voice the way she intended for each of them to sound (i.e., the deep, raspy voice of the woman in the iguana hat), she nonetheless enjoyed working on the audio version since she often performs readings of her work in front of live audiences as part of her book presentations.

Unlike the novel per se, the audio version received mixed reviews. Ann Burns condemns the project and criticizes its intent to portray a multigenerational story while shifting back and forth between characters at different points in their lives. Burns concludes that the novel's audio version "ultimately falls short" due to its "lack of a good story to tell" and insists that "these tapes require one's full attention, but the tale (with much repetition and snail-paced progression, hence little drama) refuses to captivate."[9] Burns also regards the over-dramatized nature of the audio and highlights the drawbacks of Cisneros' voice, which "rises and falls, attempting in vain to re-create each character's emotions," while recommending that a "severely abridged" version of the nearly 450-page novel might make it more enjoyable.[10]

Keir Graff has a different take on the novel's audio version. Graff praises Cisneros' voice, which he claims "ranges from soft to ebullient, and she is never afraid to growl or even shout if the passage demands it," and commends her shift between languages by asserting that "the Spanish asides that could trip other readers flow naturally here."[11] He concludes that "it is hard to imagine anyone but Cisneros bringing as much feeling to this very personal work."[12] Similar accolades for the audio version appeared in a *Publishers Weekly* review, which praised Cisneros' "ability to make listeners laugh out loud with her humor, get lumps in their throats with her poignancy and leave them thinking about her characters long after they've hit the stop button."[13] Overall, the novel *Caramelo* (both the book and the audio version) has been one of the most publicly disseminated literary projects of Cisneros' career.

Cisneros attributes the origins of her book to her desire to commemorate her father's life, a life full of struggle and perseverance emblematic of the Chicano/a immigrant community at large. Yet as the writing developed, the work took on other dimensions. In an interview with Ray Suárez, Cisneros points out:

> I didn't think I was going to be writing a history book. I thought I was writing a story about my father, based on my father's life. But in telling my father's story, I had to place him in time and history, and then I had to go back and look at how he became who he was. So I had to invent my grandmother's story and how she became who she was, so next thing I knew, there was a lot of tributaries from my main story, and footnotes, chronologies, and things like that, that I didn't antici- pate when I began.[14]

Cisneros is likewise critical of the fact that the stories of men like her father are generally undervalued or, at the most, nonexistent in the larger American social and historical context. Her intent in writing the book stems from her dis- may over the generalized perception that "his life didn't count. . . . He served in World War II, but people don't think of men like my father when they think about American history. That hurt me very deeply, to have someone I cared about so much erased and forgotten once he died, as if he meant nothing. . . . It became not just my father's story but that of all immigrants."[15]

Writing *Caramelo* took nine years in the making. The final product is a fam- ily saga that covers different incidents in the lives of four generations of a Mexican and Mexican American family and merges this history with the socio- political relations between Mexico and the United States. The work also brings to the forefront a host of cultural icons from both worlds and their factual or imaginary interaction with the characters who make up the novel. Loosely autobiographical but, like the *The House on Mango Street,* ultimately a fictional work,[16] *Caramelo* takes the reader on a nonlinear, convoluted journey through time and space that parallels the maturation process of the main narrator, Celaya Reyes, in an anecdotal yet sometimes poetic rendition of events. For Cisneros, the nine years spent on this project seemed to slip by quickly. Yet she also admits feeling relief when the process was finally over:

> There were many years when I was not so sure whether I was going to have to throw the whole thing away because I'd get very depressed. It was a nine-year process, and only in the seventh year did the pieces start to fall together. . . . I was just writing based on memory and intuition.[17]

Writer and critic Ilán Stavans comments that "genealogy rules Latino liter- ature tyrannically," and, for many authors, "fiction is a devise used to explore roots."[18] Though he objects to the proliferation of family sagas at the hands of Latino/a writers ("how many more . . . family trees are the readers capable of handling?"), he praises Cisneros' work as "brave, kaleidoscopic and ambi- tious" in its "inventive, irreverent use of the English language" and "succinct, impressionistic imagery."[19] Though the novel is an intense volume with approximately 450 pages including a chronology (longer than any of Cisneros' previous works), and covers over a century of history, the reading from one chapter to the next flows constantly with chapters "so condensed, so meteoric, they feel like snapshots arranged in a family album."[20] Like much of the writing of other Chicanas, it takes on the patterns of a Mexican *telenovela* that keeps luring the reader back to the telling of events. In other words, Lala (the main narrator) becomes "a present-day Sheherazade, and Caramelo is her Thousand and One Nights."[21] Creating Lala's character was also spurred by Cisneros' interaction with family members:

> The older I got and the more people recognized me as the writer, family stories started getting passed down to me, memoirs, a little bit of gossip, this and that. And I found myself drawing from families' *memorias,* their memoirs, as well as doing some research by doing interviews with the real people, the walking Smithsonians as I like to put it.[22]

The novel's literary genesis began as a short story meant to be published in her collection *Woman Hollering Creek and Other Stories* but was eventually left out of the work. Cisneros states:

> The story of *Caramelo* started with a memory—of a trip we took when I was a child, to Acapulco, and of a little mulatta girl I saw on the street as we walked to the beach. And I asked myself, why did this little girl stay in my memories for so many years? I mean I only saw her for a few seconds. So the question was—why did this stray memory of a girl with skin the color of *caramelo* lodge itself in my heart all these years, why was it important?[23]

Inspired by the people and incidents in her life that move her emotionally, Cisneros embarked on a fictional re-creation of this initial image, to which she claims she owes the work's title,[24] and merged the storytelling with her father's life within the historical and cultural context of two nations. Yet more than just a rendition of family history (both factual and fictional), the novel also presents, in the words of Bill Johnson González, "the clash between the values of diasporic Mexican Americans and the traditional mores and attitudes of the Mexican middle class. . . . The novel seeks to interrogate, rather than preserve, the traditional norms of Mexican culture and in particular to reveal the exclusions and repressions by means of which those norms are secured."[25]

The novel consists of three parts, eighty-six chapters and a "Pilón" chapter at the end that expresses Cisneros' gratitude to her readers for accepting her work, much like a grocer's gift of appreciation thrown in a customer's bag (in the Latino/a tradition) for patronizing his/her store. The first hard-cover edition did not include an index. This divisional construction, found in the work's subsequent printing, is highly important, according to Gabriella Gutiérrez y Muhs, for two particular reasons: "it creates an interconnected mystery for the reader" while "it de-individualizes the novel and makes all the parts of the book intrinsic parts of the various lives of the protagonists, none more or less important than the other, like a communal extended family."[26] Gutiérrez y Muhs considers the appearance of an index in later paperback editions as "an attempt to 'undiversify' Cisneros' initial intention for mystery."[27] In her opinion, this attempt works against the author's creative process and her original intent at narrative interconnection.

Caramelo opens with the main narrator, Celaya "Lala" Reyes, contemplating a family photo of a childhood trip to Acapulco. Lala bemoans the fact that she was left out of the picture: "It's as if I didn't exist. It's as if I'm the photographer walking along the beach with a tripod camera on my shoulders asking,—*¿Un recuerdo?* A souvenir? A memory?"[28] This section also initiates a recurrent leitmotif in Cisneros' work: including excerpts from popular songs (usually ballads or *rancheras*), poems, idiomatic expressions, etc., in the form of epigraphs, as integral parts of the chapter, or cited in the construction of footnotes throughout the work that reflect her knowledge of Mexican and American iconoclastic figures. Regarding the footnotes, Cisneros comments:

> I know all this trivia and I don't know where I get it and sometimes you'll ask me where I got it from and I can't even remember. But I thought a good place to put it was in the footnotes. I ran away with the footnotes. Some people enjoyed the footnotes. Some people didn't want the footnotes there. But you don't have to read the footnotes. I think no matter what you do you can't please everybody. You have to ask yourself, "Did I do what I set out to do?"[29]

Cisneros also includes cameos of legendary or commemorative figures who interact with the characters in her novel (Josephine Baker and Wenceslao Moreno, among others) as well as famous personalities from both past and present Mexican and American pop culture (Agustín Lara, María Félix, Elvis Presley, Tongolele, Lola Beltrán, Tin Tan, etc.). She also juxtaposes images of the Mexican Revolution and Mexican American War with specific references to President Woodrow Wilson, Pancho Villa, the Zapatistas, the Carranzistas, the Texas Rangers, among others, that form part of the disarray of economic and political relationships between the two countries often involving reactionary military force on both sides of the border.

Cisneros precisely credits her bilingual, bicultural upbringing and her constant commutes back and forth across the U.S.–Mexico border with providing this rich, eclectic source of knowledge, ideas, and thematic concerns that surface in her writing. Cisneros asserts:

> I have a unique perspective as the daughter of a Mexican national and a Mexican American woman. . . . I have invented a golden era of Mexico that never existed. It's a romanticized, nostalgic Mexico that the immigrant creates from a distance. We have an imaginary homeland that we see in movies and Mexican folk art and sugary Mexican songs. It's kind of this place that is neither here nor there.[30]

After the introductory section that reveals Lala's tongue-in-cheek appreciation of the family photo, Chapter 1 ("Verde, Blanco y Colorado") begins with

Lala's narration of the Reyes' annual road trip from their homes in Chicago to the grandmother's house on Destiny Street, Mexico City. The next twenty chapters display most of the characters who make up the work by focusing on family interaction once the different members cross south of the border into the paternal grandmother's (Soledad Reyes) domain. Lala refers to her as "the Awful Grandmother" throughout the novel. Thus begins the intricate weaving of family histories—some more flattering and sympathetic than others—that the narrator re-creates throughout the work.

Three main families converge in this section: Lala's immediate family made up of her parents (Inocencio and Zoila) and her brothers (Rafael, Refugio, Gustavo, Alberto, Lorenzo, and Guillermo) who all have shortened family nicknames (Rafa, Ito, Tikis, Toto, Lolo, and Memo). Inocencio's two other brothers and their families make up the other relatives: Federico and Licha with their children Elvis, Aristotle, and Byron; and Uncle Baby and Aunty Ninfa with their daughters Amor and Paz. In Mexico these families interact with the grandparents (Soledad and Narciso) and with Inocencio's sister, Norma, and her daughter Antonieta Araceli. They also interact with the family's maid, Oralia, and the washerwoman, Amparo, and her daughter Candelaria, whose skin is the color of "*caramelo.* A color so sweet, it hurts to even look at her" (37). So the reader discovers that Chapter 10 simply titled "The Girl Candelaria" pays homage to the mulatta girl whom Cisneros remembers from her trip to Acapulco whose image remained with her throughout the years. In terms of the characterization, Cisneros states: "I actually wanted to admit that characters were based on real people. But I wanted to also say and be truthful that it's based on real people but it isn't autobiography. . . . So much of the plot was invented. Even if the characters are not."[31]

The first complication that arises in Part One gives way to a detour in the narration of events in the novel. It is still the story of the family's summer commute from Chicago and its arrival at the grandmother's house in Mexico, but now the action focuses on the problems that result from the grandmother's overt preference for her eldest child, Inocencio (Lala's father). In fleshing out the father's and the grandmother's characters, Cisneros relies on her convictions regarding Mexican family relationships. She remarks:

> True love in Mexico isn't between lovers; it's between a parent and a child. Mexico is a very intense culture of sons adoring their mothers, and this is why I claim that Mexican culture is matriarchal. Because the one constant, faithful, inviolable, holy love of loves—the love of your life—is not your wife or your lover; it's your mother. . . . The wife can never compete with the mother. . . . Whatever bravado Mexican culture may have, its macho society, is created from a matriarchal culture. What's fascinating is to see this incredible reverence and admiration and exaggeration of love between a mother and a son.[32]

This understanding of love between a mother and her son lies at the heart of Inocencio's interaction with his mother, Soledad Reyes, which immediately complicates all other family relationships in the novel, particularly the one between Inocencio and his wife Zoila. Lala, the ever observant narrator, picks up on this tension and initially unspoken (yet later overtly verbal) war between the two important female figures in Inocencio's life. Thus Lala's depiction of Soledad as the Awful Grandmother stems from the fissures in their family dynamics and interaction.

These moments of tension, however, move the narrator closer to a more judicious depiction of the grandmother figure through a process of deep introspection. The major issues Cisneros constantly struggled with during the writing of the novel were how to humanize the grandmother figure, trace the developmental process that made her the woman she turned out to be, and, most importantly, explain the strong filial bond and devoted love between the grandmother and the father when she was such a detestable figure to the rest of the family. For answers to these questions, Cisneros turned to memories of her own grandmother and relied on the stories of other family members who had actual run-ins with her real-life grandmother. In the merging of fact and fiction and the process of creating her character, Cisneros undergoes a personal transformation in her realization of the significance of her own grandmother's (as well as the fictional character's) presence in the family.

Despite the grandmother's possessive nature and absolute control over the son's actions and reactions during the course of events in the novel; despite her constant bickering with the grandchildren's barbarous behavior as a result of their upbringing on the other side of the border; despite her vicious insinuations and insidious treatment of her daughter-in-law (Zoila), and her subsequent marginalization of the other sons and their families; Cisneros manages to humanize the grandmother figure and re-create (through the juxtaposition of fact and fiction) her developmental process. Cisneros scrutinized the reasons behind the grandmother's erratic behavior by focusing on the events and people that shaped the character's life. In so doing, the parallels between Cisneros' own life and her writing craft came full circle as she admits in the following statements:

> When I was writing the book, she [the grandmother] would start appearing in my face. I'm not just speaking metaphorically, I mean literally. I would look in the mirror, and her face would be there. . . . What she told me was, " . . . we are our ancestors, including the ones we don't like. . . ." Once I knew that as an author, then I could start being more generous with her as a character. . . . Therefore, the book took me to a real spiritual place. . . . [33]

Another significant complication that arises in Part One, aside from the grandmother's preferential treatment of her eldest son, takes place in the last chapter titled "Echando Palabras," regarding Candelaria's character. From the previous chapter, Lala notices a certain resemblance shared by herself, her father, and Candelaria. As the family says goodbye to Candelaria and her mother, Amparo, who have shared a family trip to Acapulco with them and the grandmother, Lala suddenly notices her mother Zoila's erratic, hysterical behavior. What follows is a violent exchange between both parents. The mother threatens to jump from the car if the father doesn't pull over and completely unsettles the rest of the passengers in the station wagon. The children, oblivious to the actual reasons behind their mother's violent outburst and insults against their father, are left caught in the middle of the verbal crossfire. Once she steps out of the car, Zoila causes a scene in front of all the bystanders in the small town through which they traveled, much to the grandmother's chagrin. Then, Zoila suddenly forces her husband to decide: either he continues his trip with her and the children or with his mother. The situation is further complicated by the grandmother's insistent plea: "*Mijo* . . . let her be. You're better off without her kind. Wives come and go, but mothers, you have only one!" (85). Suddenly the grandmother and Zoila are involved in an array of violent accusations and offenses against each other, which culminates in a standoff between the two and places the father in the middle of the decision-making process. Though the chapter ends without explicit references to his course of action, the writing reveals the family's utter shock at the father's seemingly unexpected behavior.

It is not until Part Three, "The Eagle and the Serpent or My Mother and My Father," that the mystery is solved when the father reveals: "it was you and the kids I drove home, remember? I left my own mother in Acapulco. . . . It was *you* I chose. Over my own mother! No Mexican man would choose his wife over his own mother! What more do you want? Blood?" (235). With this narration of events, Cisneros confirms that hers will be a story of dialectic difference, of changing realities, reconceptualizing family relationships, confronting cultural mores, and creating strategic encounters that question the very essence of cultural and gendered presumptions. Though the father still empathizes with his mother, his wife has clearly won this battle.

Before arriving at this realization in Part Three, the mid section of the book titled "When I Was Dirt" takes the reader on a crusade centered on the grandmother's character and her development within a historical/cultural context. Part Two focuses on the grandmother's upbringing (raised by her father's cousin, Fina, after her mother Guillermina's death and her widowed father Ambrosio's second marriage) and then Soledad's subsequent marriage to Narciso Reyes, son of Eleuterio and Regina Reyes. This part is preceded by a section that explains the title's origins as a famous introductory line that signals the telling of events before the narrator's time ("when I was dirt"). Cisneros takes advantage of this resource to give further insights and to justify Lala's narration. The line also imbues the narrator with certain privileged information, particularly regarding events that happened before she was even born. This information comes primarily through family history and the oral tradition passed down through generations. But the stories are also enhanced by Lala's creative imagination and her re-creation of events as she imagined they occurred.

Yet what makes this part of the work stand out from the other two parts is the new twist in narrative discourse that the author employs. Though the main

narration predominantly remains in Lala's character, there are sporadic inter-
ruptions, written in bold print, that belong to the grandmother. Her commentary, suggestions, and contradictions lend a different dimension to what has
otherwise been Lala's one-sided storytelling. The combination of narrative
voices is a fascinating exchange/narrative dialogue between granddaughter and
grandmother that cuts to the core of literary representation. It is in this section
that the grandmother is most humanized, most vulnerable, and vividly characterized. It is also through Lala's understanding of the ambivalence of her
grandmother's life that she comes to terms with her own relationship to this
otherwise contradictory, obstinate, but ultimately strong and determined
female character. In turn, the grandmother also learns a valuable lesson: that
she urgently needs Lala's intervention to set the record straight and that by
revealing her life story, Lala participates in a revindication of her family history.
In other words, Lala, and not the grandmother, controls the narration of
events. It is ultimately through Lala's eyes, her perceptions, and her voice that
the narration unfolds, with all its twists and turns, and all the references to historical events and cultural icons real or imagined. Yet the reader must also
acknowledge that the narrator constantly admits to lapses of memory, poor
judgment, and narrative incongruity.

Part Three ultimately reveals Lala's understanding and acceptance of her
grandmother:

> It hits me at once, the terrible truth of it. I am the Awful Grandmother. . . . I've
> turned into her. And I see inside her heart, the Grandmother, who has been
> betrayed so many times she only loves her son. He loves her. And I love him. I
> have to find room inside my heart for her as well, because she holds him inside
> her heart like when she held him inside her womb, the clapper inside a bell. . . .
> Maybe it's my job to separate the strands [of the rebozo] and knot the words
> together for everyone who can't say them, and make it all right in the end.
> (424–425, 428)

Whereas Part One presents the narrator engulfed in the world south of the
border where the grandmother rules and Lala feels like an intruder, Part Two
concentrates on the development of the grandmother's character. Part Three,
on the other hand, shifts the setting north of the border where the family has
returned to the habitual surroundings of Chicago, albeit with the grandmother
in tow after the grandfather's sudden death in Mexico. Part Three also shifts
the focus of narration back to Lala and her interaction with other family members, particularly her rendition of her parents' courtship and marriage and the
family's constant moving from one home to the next. There are no other inter-
ventions or narrative dialogues between Lala and the grandmother like the
ones seen in Part Two. Lala turns to depictions of her father's struggles as a
Mexican immigrant trying to make a living in the upholstery business. She also
scrutinizes her mother's growing discontent when she (Zoila) experiences a
sense of stagnation, as if her life were slipping through her hands.

Another important aspect of Part Three is that it brings to the forefront intracultural confrontations between Mexicans and Mexican Americans. These confrontations are spurred by preconceptions on both sides of the border regarding cultural affiliations and authenticity. Mexicans often look down on immigrants who leave the country, who assimilate to North American society, and condemn them as "sell-outs," or traitors. Mexican immigrants who have made a life in the United States frequently see their fellow Mexicans south of the border as too traditional and "backwards," unwilling to change and follow social modernization movements and progressive ideologies.

Throughout the narration, a cultural and linguistic schism arises among those still living in Mexico, those who immigrated to the United States but still identify as Mexican, those who identify as Mexican American, and/or those who are more assimilated to Anglo American culture derisively known as "Pochos." For the most part, the grandmother expresses strong contempt for anyone living outside of Mexico and for those who fail to adhere to strict Mexican cultural mores that extend to speaking the mother tongue, Spanish. To a certain extent, this antagonistic sentiment is passed on to her son, Inocencio, but is immediately confronted by his wife Zoila's Mexican American upbringing, lifestyle, and linguistic adherence to English. Thus, the grandmother regards her son's family as barbarians. Lala's description of the grandmother in the following scene addresses this issue: "the Awful Grandmother herself has seen how these children raised on the other side don't know enough to answer,—*¿Mande usted?* to their elders.—What? we say in the horrible language, which the Awful Grandmother hears as *¿Guat?*— The Awful Grandmother shakes her head and mutters,—My daughters-in-law have given birth to a generation of monkeys" (28).

Yet in Chapter 56 titled "The Man From Mars," Lala's father, Inocencio, confronts this embedded intracultural resistance when he interacts with Marcelino "Mars" Ordóñez, his friend while serving in World War II and current owner of a small *taquería* where the family stops for dinner in San Antonio on its trip back to Chicago. Inocencio describes his friend's spontaneous generosity when he (Inocencio) was once left stranded with no money in New Orleans. Mars gave Inocencio $50 from his wallet to help Inocencio get by under the pretext that they were "familia" and "raza." Most surprisingly, especially to Lala, is what happens next:

> Then Mars does the funky *raza* handshake with Father, like Chicano power, and Father, who is always ranting and raving about Chicanos, the same Father who calls Chicanos *exagerados, vulgarones,* zoot-suiting, wild-talking, forget-they-were-Mexican Mexicans, surprised us all. Father handshakes the funky handshake back. (280–281)

Inocencio later has a run-in with Mars over business issues, but his perception of Mexican Americans changes throughout the course of the novel, just like Lala's observations gather more and more details regarding the intraracial conflicts and intricate coexistence of those who live on opposite sides of the border. In fact, these same contradictions spark Lala's interest, especially when she meets a new classmate, Viva Ozuna, who identifies as Mexican, but surprises Lala by revealing that she's never actually been to Mexico. Lala internalizes the conflicts related to identity and cultural loyalties that many immigrants, particularly Mexicans, experience as they interact with others. As Johnson González rightfully points out, "the novel is overflowing with examples of the Mexican middle-class's ideologies of racial hatred, articulated in common speech."[34] Thus the grandmother, among other characters, derisively refers to working-class Mexicans as "Indians," judging them by their darker skin color, while positioning herself within a separate social and racial privileged class. Lala, on the other hand, sees through this posturing, especially when she finds out that the grandmother's family is not as economically well off as she thought it to be and particularly when Lala notices the myriad complexions of the Mexican people. This realization is particularly evident during the family's move to a new home in Texas and Lala has to confront the rejection of her new classmates:

> A part of me feels sorry for their stupid ignorant selves. But if you've never been farther south than Nuevo Laredo, how the hell would you know what Mexicans are supposed to look like. There are the green-eyed Mexicans. The rich blonde Mexicans. The Mexicans with the faces of Arab sheiks. The Jewish Mexicans. The big-footed-as-a-German Mexicans. The leftover-French Mexicans. The *chaparrito* compact Mexicans. . . . The Mediterranean Mexicans. The Mexicans with Tunisian eyebrows. The *negrito* Mexicans of the double coasts. . . . Look, I don't know what you're talking about when you say I don't look Mexican. I *am* Mexican. Even though I was born on the U.S. side of the border. (352–353)

Far from dwelling on identity crises and cultural disloyalties, Lala develops her own tactics for surviving between and within both worlds, what Gloria Anzaldúa refers to as "a *mestiza* consciousness:"

> The new *mestiza* copes by developing a tolerance for contradictions, a tolerance for ambiguity. . . . She learns to juggle cultures. She has a plural personality, she operates in a pluralistic mode—nothing is thrust out, the good the bad and the ugly, nothing rejected, nothing abandoned. Not only does she sustain contradictions, she turns the ambivalence into something else.[35]

Through her maturation process, through her amalgamation of both languages (Spanish and English), and through her exposure to Mexican and Anglo American culture and society, Lala is able to analyze and question the foundations that underpin cultural mores and practices in both settings. She also avoids the glamorization of one culture over the other by showcasing both their strengths and weaknesses, which surprisingly reveals a balanced interaction between cultures. In so doing, Lala is able to lift the veil of prejudice that imbues characters like her grandmother and move beyond racist and classicist concepts of identification. As a result, Lala appreciates Candelaria's beauty, for instance, primarily based on her skin color: "The girl Candelaria has skin bright as the copper *veinte centavos* coin after you've sucked it. . . . Not like anybody. Smooth as peanut butter, deep as burnt-milk candy" (34), even though the image of Candelaria plays against traditional, imbedded notions of beauty (Lala's Aunty Light-Skin or women on televised beauty contests).

While the title initially refers to Candelaria's character, it then takes on different dimensions throughout the novel. At one point the title refers to a specific pattern used in the making of *rebozos.* One of the novel's stylistic accomplishments is precisely how Cisneros manages to weave, literally and metaphorically speaking, the making of a *caramelo rebozo* with Soledad Reyes' characterization. The last footnote in Chapter 21 highlights the history of the *rebozo,* which the narrator insists was:

> born in Mexico, but like all *mestizos,* it came from everywhere. It evolved from the cloths Indian women used to carry their babies, borrowed its knotted fringe from the Spanish shawls, and was influenced by the silk embroideries from the imperial court of China exported to Manila, then Acapulco, via the Spanish galleons. (96)

The *rebozo,* aside from its eclectic and humble origins, becomes an essential symbol for Mexican women who used it for various purposes (as adornment, to carry children, as head covering in a church, as umbrella or parasol, a modest covering while breast-feeding, etc.). They ranged in elegance and style from those used on a daily basis made of common, less expensive materials to silk *rebozos* of elaborate designs primarily worn on special occasions such as weddings. The *rebozo* also becomes a symbol that links the grandmother, Soledad, to her own mother who passed away when Soledad was a child. Soledad's only inheritance and memory of her mother (Guillermina) was an intricately elaborated *caramelo rebozo* that Guillermina left unfinished. Another person cannot complete the stitching without undoing the whole *rebozo* so Soledad keeps it intact in honor of her mother's crafty and delicate art work. Until her own death, the grandmother keeps this *rebozo* locked up as a precious item in an old armoire that migrates with her to the United States.

Gutiérrez y Muhs sees the *rebozo* as "a symbol for the four cultures that make up the protagonists in the novel. . . . What the unfinished rebozo represents is the cultural syncretism weaved into the family's history."[36] In other words, the intricate patterns of the *caramelo rebozo* that no one can finish is much like the story of Lala's life and her generation, influenced by Mexican and Mexican American matriarchal figures yet existing in their own right. As Gutiérrez y Muhs aptly concludes, "the rebozo represents the unfulfilled/incomplete life of the Awful Grandmother and the possible future life of Celaya, a historical mantelpiece of her fire. At the end of the road, Celaya understands that she and the Grandmother are very similar, moreover expressing the circularity of the novel, in part through the metaphor of the rebozo."[37]

For Cisneros, the act of writing *Caramelo,* and interpreting the metaphorical symbolism of the *rebozo* in these terms, becomes a means through which she can merge all the important aspects of her life: history, culture, language, family, storytelling, imagination, memoir. In many ways, it is a powerfully gifted and crafted tool that she utilizes in order to make sense and reconcile the multiple layers of her *mestiza* subjectivity and in so doing pay homage to the significant people that share her life or that creatively inhabit her fictional world. As Ellen McCracken accurately points out, "*Caramelo* brings together aesthetic nuances, post-modern experimentation, pleasurable images of ethnicity, linguistic play, humor, and new points of entry into history to create a compelling family saga that offers readers many sites of identification. The novel marks Cisneros' definitive entry into the U.S. literary canon."[38]

Nevertheless, Cisneros arrived at the end of her work with a certain degree of apprehension. She somehow coalesced the actual finishing of the text with her father's final days:

> When I won the McArthur [Foundation Award] I had this horrible feeling that my father was going to die. . . . My father got sick last autumn [1997] and he had a quadruple bypass, and I was sure he was not going to survive it. It was a few months after the McArthur, and I said well, here it comes. . . . His health has been failing. I believe there's something bigger, that a much more incredible Author than I'll ever be arranged things in an incredible pattern. I knew when the McArthur came that my father was going to be taken. It was just time.[39]

Known as "the genius grants," the MacArthur Foundation[40] is one of the largest multibillion private philanthropic foundations that supports and fosters individual creativity while it strengthens and improves public policy with a particular commitment to diversity. Aside from providing a sense of validation and public recognition for her work in larger literary circles, winning the MacArthur Award also took on a personal dimension for Cisneros when it allowed her the freedom and economic stability to work on her most ambitious project, her novel *Caramelo,* on the one hand, and also to be with her father during his illness.

Because of Cisneros' close relationship to her father, his illness became a particularly trying time for her. Sheltered within his overprotective love and accustomed to his lyrical, crooning voice, which she identified so much as part of their Mexicanness, Cisneros' father was always "the popular parent," someone she considered almost soft and feminine while her mother took on the role of the sterner, disciplinary parent. Watching her father succumb to his disease was devastating for Cisneros, yet at the same time she managed to turn it into a valuable learning experience that would guide her life and her writing. In an emotionally telling interview with Bridget Kevane and Juanita Heredia,[41] Cisneros comments on what this process meant to her and how she came to terms with her father's death:

> When you ask for spiritual growth, you better believe it is some horrible pain that is going to happen in your life. It's always like when the shamans have their forty days in the desert. Horrible, horrible experiences that are going to take you

to another level of spiritual awareness. I knew I needed them for the stories I had to tell, and then, of course, the most traumatic things in my life happened. My father is diagnosed with cancer and I watch him die. . . . Yet how lucky that I am a writer! I can muddle through. It's having a knife pulled out of your eye. . . . I think writers are always split between living their life and watching themselves live it. . . . Unless you lose someone you are very close to, you cannot know what other people are talking about. It connects you to humanity. . . . Since my father died, it has brought a lot of things into focus. I am living more intensely as a result of my father dying. This is the book that is meant for me to write right now, to take me through this period of having to let my father go. The death of my father was just extraordinary. I think part of me knew that I could not finish the book until my father died, that there was some way that my father was going to help me write the book. He certainly has been there for me since his passing.[42]

Moreover, she was proud of the fact that her father lived long enough to understand and respect the work that she does. In an interview with Jen Buckendorff, Cisneros remarks on the ways in which her parents, particularly her father, reacted toward her accomplishments and awards by stating that:

What made him [father] actually understand that I was indeed a professional writer was two things: one was the MacArthur, not because he understood what the MacArthur was, but because he understood the amount ($250,000). The other thing was that he saw Carlos Fuentes on Spanish-language TV and Carlos Fuentes mentioned my name as one of the writers he admires. That my father understood.[43]

Yet despite the fact that the novel is about a particular Mexican and Mexican American family, many readers are finding hints of their own family or family circumstances in it, as Cisneros is constantly reminded during her book presentations and readings. Regarding reader reception, Cisneros comments:

If you are Mexican, they feel like crying because they feel no one has written about this and they are emotionally overwhelmed. If you are of another culture . . . you will come up surprised and say, "Well, I'm Persian but this could have been my family." People from very different cultures than mine see themselves in this book. Even the most *gringo* gringo . . . will be laughing at the appropriate moment. I think there is a place for them even though it is specifically about a culture that is unlike my listeners. . . . You know, you make it so specific that it does that little paradox of becoming universal.[44]

Additional plans for *Caramelo* include transforming it into a film because of its cinematic qualities. For Cisneros, however, the best adaptation of her work should come in the form of a *telenovela*, not a two-hour feature, but one that can be showcased both in the United States and in Mexico, so that all viewers would be able to experience the rich array of historical, cultural, and linguistic ingredients that make up Mexican and Mexican American immigrant reality and hybridity.

With *Caramelo,* Cisneros leaves a lasting imprint on the world of American letters. The universal quality of her writing and her conscientious intent to bring to the forefront the stories of those who make up and participate in the American social fabric (though still often ignored or remaining on the periphery), place her writing among the most influential voices of the twenty-first century. Her work reminds us, in the words of Virginia Brackett, "that our humanity connects us, despite differences in skin color, religion, or birthplace, and that we all must tell our own stories to deepen that connection."[45]

FIVE

A Rebellious Soul in San Antonio: Sandra Cisneros' Social Activism

Print articulation alone cannot fully represent the co-motion of culture; it reminds us again that existence should never be reduced to language alone, that cultural literacy should never be exclusively based in literature per se and, consequently, that cultural critics—and their critiques—should get out and dance a bit more often.

—Lisa Sánchez-González, *Boricua Literature*

Sandra Cisneros' literary career spans well over two decades since the publication of her first works of poetry and fiction. Recipient of numerous grants and fellowships and winner of prestigious literary awards, Cisneros has garnered a reputation as one of the leading literary voices of contemporary American letters and has become a widely read and critically acclaimed author. Along with this recognition as a major literary figure comes a sense of cultural awareness and social activism that, for the most part, characterizes her writing and lies at the heart of her emergence as an author committed to the advancement of social justice and equal rights, particularly in the Latino communities that nurtured her upbringing and that constantly sustain her artistic creativity.

Cisneros' development of a social consciousness began early in life as she formed part of a working-class family of Mexican immigrants (on her father's side) and Mexican American heritage (on her mother's side). Primarily sheltered within this Mexican American household full of brothers and an over-protective father who frequently moved his family between Mexico and the United States, Cisneros learned to observe, at an early age and with keen precision, the nuances of distinct (and often overtly oppositional) cultural and linguistic practices. In order to survive in this constant *vaivén*,[1] Cisneros had to negotiate these divergent binaries in a process of *amasamiento*[2] that would ensure her social transitions in both geographic spaces and that would ultimately enable her safe (albeit tense or precarious) transit in Anglo American settings. This constant shifting back and forth between geographic borders, however, is more intrinsically related to her formative years since Cisneros' family eventually opted for less frequent transnational crossings in lieu of more permanent living arrangements within the United States, a movement certainly more characteristic of Cisneros' young adult and adult life.

As discussed in previous chapters, Cisneros' awakening to a world of insider-outsider status where class, race, and ethnicity determined, and to a large extent governed, quotidian reality began with her participation in the University of Iowa Writers Workshop. Her sense of displacement and underprivileged position spurred her artistic creativity and through a haze of indignant fury and outrage she began to produce some of her finest work. In her attempts to write from the familiar space of her Mexican American corporeality, a space seemingly unbeknownst to and intrinsically detached from the lives of the majority of her fellow classmates at Iowa, Cisneros delved into the core of what would later turn out to be her literary trademark: an unwavering, socially conscientious commitment to her roots, though at times it has required a confrontation and/or questioning of the same cultural ties and practices she claims to withhold both in her life and in her writing.

Another important locus of social awareness for Cisneros was her experience after graduating from the workshop and returning to Chicago. When she moved back to what she claims was an unrecognizable city compared with the one she originally left behind, Cisneros began to associate with other artists through MARCH (*Movimiento Artístico Chicano*). She did not always agree with the artists' work ethics and often frowned upon their lack of technical self-discipline, which she considered unprofessional and at opposite ends with her rigorous training at the Writers Workshop. Yet, in time, she learned to reexamine her definition of poetics as she took into consideration the fact that her academic training exposed her to a larger corpus of writing and poetic skills than was the case of her fellow writers in the movement. It was also through MARCH that she was able to connect to job placements, and this was how she came upon the Latino Youth Alternative High School. Working with the staff and youth at this small community school located in the Mexican *barrio* that catered primarily to high school drop-outs forever changed Cisneros' outlook on education and the roles that class and privilege play in the completion of any academic degree. Of her experience at the Alternative High School, Cisneros comments:

I suppose working with this progressive staff shaped my political ideology and gave me a sense of direction and roots. All of a sudden I was traveling through the alleys and back ways of ghetto and gutter, a tattered country-side of brick and broken glass and the rumbling el trains overhead. All the world shook with city-soot and pigeon-dust. It was a strange re-awakening from the timid past. . . . It was during these three years that my sense of identification and social concern and commitment developed.[3]

Cisneros' involvement with the students resulted in significant developments and improvements to the school's arts component and provided her students with a helpful and much-needed artistic and creative outlet to confront the harsh environment and living conditions that surrounded them. Cisneros points out that "it was my students' appreciation and awareness of the arts that was my consolation during these exhausting times."[4] During her years at the Latino Alternative High School, Cisneros also managed to bring in grants from the Illinois and Chicago arts councils, which helped her teach creative writing and assisted in financing other artists to come to the school. Slowly but surely the school's credibility with state and city arts agencies grew, which guaranteed yearly funding. Cisneros' social commitment also extended beyond the school to conducting free workshops and poetry readings to support the cause of the sponsor, usually in the Latino or African American communities, a nonprofit agency, a woman's group, or any political group that she believed in. Much has changed since those rallying days and community-oriented duties (Cisneros now receives upwards of $10,000 for a guest appearance) but her commitment to art, culture, and Latino heritage still remain strong.

The time devoted to militant change and progressive ideologies in her years at the Latino Alternative High School and her subsequent employment as assistant to the director of the Educational Opportunity Program at Loyola University (1980–1981) frequently prevented Cisneros from dedicating herself entirely to writing. Receiving her first National Endowment of the Arts Award in 1982 provided the much-needed space and economic support to pursue her writing full-time. Receiving this award resulted not only in the completion and publication of her first work (*The House on Mango Street*), but also opened the door to future grants and awards (among them a second NEA, the Dobie Paisano Fellowship, the Anisfield-Wolf Book Award, the Lannan Foundation Literary Award, the Before Columbus American Book Award, and a MacArthur Fellowship). Arriving at a point in her literary career where she could make a living off her writing began with her connection to literary agent, Susan Bergholz, and her six-digit advance from Random House Publishers for *Woman Hollering Creek* in 1987. Since then Cisneros has steadily produced an increasing corpus of literary works and simultaneously solidified her reputation as a feisty feminist Chicana committed to revolution and social change.

One instance in which Cisneros proved her staunch allegiance to the Latino/a community occurred in 1992 when an agent from the retail clothing store The Gap approached her to film several commercials sponsoring the store and promoting their products. This also meant working with acclaimed photographer Annie Leibovitz as part of the contract. Though the offer was quite lucrative and promised increased exposure for Cisneros, she refused to accept on the grounds that The Gap had failed to use other Latino/a representatives for their commercials during the course of the store's development, which demonstrated, in Cisneros' opinion, the store's lack of commitment to the Latino/a community. On a similar note, a year after The Gap incident, in 1993, Cisneros was invited to a local San Antonio bookstore for a reading to promote her work. Yet she immediately confronted the bookstore owner for not supporting other Latino/a authors to do the same. She insisted that the only way she would agree to do a reading was if he invited other Latinos/as to join her.

In 1995 Cisneros participated in a film project that showcased and celebrated Southwestern woman artists. She joined Navajo poet Luci Tapahonso and their collaborative efforts with seven other women resulted in the hour-long film, *The Desert is No Lady*. Written by Susan Palmer and produced and directed by Shelley Williams for Women Make Movies,[5] the film is based in part on the 1987 Yale University Press publication *The Desert Is No Lady: Landscapes in Women's Writing and Art*. Women Make Movies is a multicultural, multiracial nonprofit media arts organization that addresses the underrepresentation of women in the film industry. The organization's main purpose is to facilitate the production, promotion, distribution, and exhibition of individual or collaborative works by and about women. The program particularly supports films by women of color and the development of a feminist media through an internationally recognized distribution service and a production assistance program. When Cisneros was approached to participate in this project, she immediately agreed in hopes of further disseminating the works of Southwestern women artists.

A total of nine women participated in the film. Along with Cisneros and Tapahonso, Chicana poet Pat Mora; the painters Emmi Whitehorse, Harmony Hammond, and Pola López de Jaramillo; photographer Meridel Rubenstein; sculptor Nora Naranjo Morse; and tapestry artist Ramona Sakiestewa, also participated. Cisneros' intervention consists of a monologue describing different aspects of her writing and her life in different parts of the United States. Regarding her experience,[6] she points out:

> I think it's especially schizophrenic for any person of color in the world to be living in a culture where your language and your culture is not the predominant one, where you don't see yourself in books or the media. I think for myself there was that split . . . especially when I lived in the Midwest, of having this private self, this private language, the language everyone spoke at home and then the public language I was educated in and the major I was educated in was English. But then, when I moved to the Southwest, what I was given permission to do from living here was to incorporate the voices I saw [sic] around me and what those voices did was to mix Spanish and English a lot more than I had ever heard

in my life. I started borrowing from the mixture of phrases that I found in this particular place, in this borderland region, and using it to inspire story titles and especially to allow the characters themselves who had never appeared in Texan literature or that never appeared in North American literature to speak through my stories.[7]

After these remarks, Cisneros reads excerpts from some of the stories in her collection *Woman Hollering Creek* and then focuses specifically on how she conceived and created one of the most well-known short stories of that series, "Eyes of Zapata." Cisneros comments: "The way I usually come to a story is by looking at my obsessions and this story, Eyes of Zapata, came to me from my own interest from photographs of Emiliano Zapata, the Mexican revolutionary leader." After conducting research on Zapata, Cisneros found "a tiny footnote" in one of the biographies that mentioned his wives. Discovering that Zapata had several wives, she decides to further investigate his common-law wife, the one he never married, but the mother of his eldest child who became a constant in his life despite his other marriages. Unfortunately, very little was actually written on this figure or on any Mexican women in general during the Revolution. "Because there is a void," Cisneros says, "there's nothing, I have to invent her story. Who could be this woman who could hold such power over such a great man? And that's where my story took flight, when I tried to create a character that would be equal in stature to a great general. Being that she is Indian and poor, the only option I had was to make her either a *puta* (a whore), or a *bruja* (a witch) and I was much more interested in a witch. So I made her into a witchwoman, a *nagual*."[8]

In several articles Cisneros comments on the metaphysical effects that writing this story produced in her when at times she often felt unable to shed the remnants of the fictional personification of Zapata's lover (Inés Alfaro). Jim Sagel sees Inés as "the woman warrior, the *Soldadera* who understands what the men will never comprehend, that 'the wars begin here, in our hearts and in our beds.' She is the *bruja,* the *nagual* who flies through the night, the fierce and tender lover who risks all, the eater of black things that make her hard and strong. She is, in short, a symbol of the Latina herself . . . whose story is at last being told, a story of life and blood and grief and 'all the flower colors of joy.' It is a story at once intimate and universal, guaranteed to shove a bittersweet thorn into the paws of literary lions everywhere."[9] Cisneros was so enraptured by the telling of events in "Eyes of Zapata," delivered in a first person narration, that she seemed to become one with Ines' character who constantly haunted Cisneros' dreams to the point that she felt she could see the historical events and surroundings that gave way to the story through Inés' eyes but in the physicality of Cisneros' own present. As Jeff Thomson rightfully points out, "when a writer claims to identify with a character to the extent that she wakes up unsure who she is, one can assume that that character is going to speak deeply and come as close to the truth as fiction can come to the truth of the human heart. This is true of Inés."[10] Inés' narration, from the gendered perspective of a wife/lover and soulmate privy to the more "humane" (i.e., insecure, frightened, vulnerable) side of Emiliano Zapata, deconstructs the myth of the Mexican hero and hypermasculine figure of the Mexican Revolution. Inés' narration also argues for the rightful place of women within the history of the Revolution as her multiple escapades alongside Zapata and other revolutionaries (particularly women) in the story attest. After reading from different segments of "Eyes of Zapata" in the film *The Desert Is No Lady,* Cisneros concludes:

> In telling these stories I aim to empower Chicana women and Mexican women. It helps to look at our past and claim some part of ourselves and to let go shame and to let go, perhaps, images of passive and helpless women and to revise them, re-look at them, as places to empower and liberate us and to rid us of detrimental emotions like shame and exchange them for something like sexual energy, sexual power, willfulness, and to see those as positive things, not as qualities one might equate with bad women.[11]

Another important aspect of Cisneros' social activism is her interest in creating spaces that nurture the creative writing process and, at the same time, cater to the needs of those untraditionally represented within the world of letters. In 1995, Cisneros founded the Macondo Workshop.[12] A unique master's level summer workshop named after the sleepy town in Gabriel García Márquez's novel, *One Hundred Years of Solitude,* the Macondo Workshop transforms San Antonio and the *frontera* into a space of intense artistic and cultural creativity. The Workshop is a gathering for writers working on geographic, cultural, social, and spiritual borders with a global sense of community and a strong spirit of generosity modeled after its founder (Cisneros) who volunteers valuable writing time for the nourishment of other writers. The participants are, in the words of Ruth Behar, "Americans of the other America, moving between cultures, languages, classes, homelands, translating our experience for ourselves and others."[13] Writers who attend this Workshop come from different parts of the United States to gather for one week of creative productivity, cultural exchange, and social commitment. Vicente Lozano describes the writers gathered for the Workshop as those who:

> have witnessed firsthand the effects of poverty, depression, incarceration, poor health, violence, and mental illness—and they feel a sense of honor and obligation to have their writing stand for something larger than individual talent. . . . Not only were people there to believe they were writers, they were there to get the energy and spirit it had taken for each person to arrive. They wanted to understand what the other was doing, and to offer what they could. . . . Generosity multiplied energy. It was practical, this indigenous Latino notion of collective responsibility.[14]

Before attending, participants are expected to have accomplished one or more of the following: published a book or several short stories in journals or magazines, enrolled in or completed an MFA program, or studied with professional writers. They may attend up to three years, but then can return as teachers or writers-in-residence. On the origins of Macondo, Cisneros comments:

> Back in 1984, as Director of the Guadalupe Arts Center, I had a dream of creating a series of workshops to help raise the level of writing, because I felt that a lot of Chicano writing I was reading suffered from being unfinished. . . . So I started a workshop as Director. It wasn't Master's level but open to anyone. Later on . . . in 1995 [in San Antonio], I volunteered and taught a Master's level workshop. They combed through and gave me maybe twenty-five manuscripts to read. The third year I wanted it to be by invitation only, so I opened it to my ex-students, including those from the Woman's Peace Center in Austin. And that was in my dinning room. The next year Arturo Madrid said we could have it at Trinity University. . . . I realized the community that I want and need, it's not in any city, I have to create it. And so I have with Macondo. When people come together for a week each summer to discuss their writing, to take it seriously, that's my homeland.[15]

Though some of the workshops literally took place in Cisneros' home, they gradually moved to different locales in the San Antonio area, such as the Esperanza Peace and Justice Center.[16] The Center is an organization that promotes social justice through cultural arts programming and advocating on behalf of people of color, women, lesbians, gay men, the working class, and the poor. The Center's main prerogative is for its attendees to learn that, in order to participate fully in democratic civic life, individuals must be culturally grounded, confident in their own voices, and certain of the value of their contributions. The Center believes that this grounding can ultimately be obtained through art and a strong sense of heritage and culture. The Macondo Workshop, then, fits appropriately into the Center's philosophy.

The application process for the Workshop is currently by invitation or through nomination by its members. Yet it has diligently worked toward its institutionalization. It is now officially considered a nonprofit organization with its own structure, mission statement, bylaws, staff, board members, and advisory board. In the years it has been operating, Cisneros has managed to bring together extraordinary groups of people, including the filmmaker Lourdes Portillo, anthropologists Renato Rosaldo and Ruth Behar, the president of the Farm Labor Organizing Committee Baldemar Velázquez, renowned fiction writers and poets (Luis Rodríguez, Denise Chávez, Alicia Gaspar de Alba, Gary Soto, Joy Harjo, and Raúl Salinas) as well as several journalists and literary agents, among others. Attendance has progressively increased over the years, from thirteen members in its initial gathering to eighty who participated in 2007. In the past years since its foundation, over 200 participants (including faculty and alumni) have shared their experience and talents, including several MacArthur Foundation Fellows and more than twenty-five published authors. Their joint efforts align with Cisneros' vision of Macondo as a space both situated in arts and politics as well as a medium through which to channel the creative writing process.

Cisneros remains loyal to the grassroots, academic, and feminist orientation that inspired the foundation of Macondo as well as to its commitment to social change. Yet she nonetheless welcomes new focuses and trends. After surveying the progress made by the workshop, she states:

> The workshop is going to keep changing. It's okay for it to change as long as it stays true to its sense of generosity, of nurturing and of feeding. As long as it has a multiplicity of backgrounds, a multiplicity of borderlands, and an integration of worldviews. . . . I don't worry about what it's becoming. We collect writers who are in it for social change.[17]

Through Macondo, Cisneros also recently established the Elvira Cordero Cisneros Award[18] in 2007 to honor her mother's memory. Recipients of this award are selected for their exceptional talents, commitment to their artistic expressions, and dedication to nurturing others' creativity. Cisneros has written, "We wanted to give it [the award] to someone who is too busy nurturing others to nurture herself. My mother was a deeply creative, but frustrated artist, and I don't want to see others live their lives with regrets for what they didn't do."[19] In a similar vein, several years before in 2000, Cisneros created the Alfredo Cisneros del Moral Foundation, a grant-giving institution serving Texas writers, to honor the memory of her father, an upholsterer. Regarding her father and the significance of this award, Cisneros has commented, "My father lived his life as an example of generosity and honest labor. . . . Even as he warned us to save our centavitos, he was always giving away his own. A meticulous craftsman, he would sooner rip the seams of a cushion apart and do it over, than put his name on an item that wasn't up to his high standards. I especially wanted to honor his memory by an award showcasing writers who are equally proud of their own craft."[20] Both awards attest not only to Cisneros' commitment to honoring the memory of her parents in particular, but also to showcasing the tenacity, hard work, and courageous spirits of the thousands of Latinos/as like them whose exemplary behavior make up the heart and soul of unsung heroes, past and present.

In addition, there is also the "Casa Azul Residency," a writer-in-residence program sponsored by the Macondo Foundation only available to Macondo Workshop members for limited time periods. Located on 736 E. Guenther Street, close to Cisneros' own house, the residency program offers "a space where Macondistas could retreat from the distractions of everyday life, a house, a room of his/her own for the process of emotional, intellectual, and spiritual introspection."[21] This program suits the needs of writers who view their work and talents as part of a larger process of community-building and social change, two major principles inherent in the foundation of Macondo and also an integral part of Cisneros' own social activism.

When Cisneros won the prestigious MacArthur Foundation Award in 1995, she decided to turn this event into a larger project that would eventually benefit the Latino/a community. Based on her experience as a MacArthur fellow, Cisneros founded "the MacArturos,"[22] a self-initiated, self-organizing collective of former MacArthur Latino/a recipients who share their creativity and expertise with a social activist agenda to inspire other Latino/a youth. The events usually included educational performances and lectures that catered to the needs of Latino communities with a mission for the members of these communities to reunite and assist one another. Their first reunion was held in San Antonio, Texas, in October 1997, led by twelve former MacArthur recipients under the title "*An Ofrenda: de Alma, Corazón y Mente*" (An Offering: From the Soul, Heart, and Mind). The subsequent plan was to meet annually in a city where one of the Latino/a MacArthur fellows lived, which took them to meetings in San José, Los Angeles, Toledo, and Chicago. Though the members eventually stopped meeting on a yearly basis, conversations initiated again for a revival. In Cisneros words, "We want[ed] to encourage local geniuses, both young and established, to brainstorm and imagine San Antonio ten years forward. We believe that uniting in this way we will be able to leave behind a legacy of ideas. It was our experience in the past that border-crossing disciplines—that is, having labor organizers mixing with performance artists, anthropologists with voting rights specialists, etc.—allowed us to see solutions to problems in new and creative ways. It is then with this dream of uniting our Locos, Dreamers, and Visionaries, local and invited, that we hope to dream a new San Antonio."[23]

These conversations gave way to a MacArturos reunion in 2007 held in its place of origin—San Antonio, Texas. Eighteen "Latino Geniuses" (as Cisneros refers to the Latino MacArthur recipients) gathered from October 4–6 and participated in gatherings at different universities, galleries, and cultural centers across the city in a series of "dream circles" that brought experts and community members together in an effort to encourage other Latino/a communities in other cities across the nation. All the events and gatherings were free and open to the public. In a Texas Public Radio News interview with Ivette Benavides, Cisneros stated that "the Latino community is in great pain and we need to bring together the healers or *curanderos* of our time, the ones who are asked to see into the past and look beyond into the future for solutions."[24] And so they met, under the common denominator of "Latin@ Geniuses: Locos, Dreamers, and Visionaries" to tackle issues affecting the Latino/a community (immigration, education, labor rights, mass media portrayal, housing and community planning, *testimonios* and songs, politics and voting, etc.). In its initial planning stages, Cisneros remarked, "maybe it is a *loco* idea to do this gathering, but it is an opportunity to dialogue, to present a different history than the official story, to talk about things important to us as opposed to what gets imposed on us by the mass media. We can create the news. And even if only two of us met, we learned, that's news. So the fact that we're going to have 18 this weekend is nothing short of historic."[25] Unlike the first MacArturos reunion, which was primarily focused on youth and intent on providing forums for their concerns, the 2007 reunion went a step further in that it addressed specific problems affecting the Latino/a community and the city at large. University of Texas professor and event co-organizer Ellen Riojas Clark and others praised Cisneros' efforts and the MacArturos' willingness to share their knowledge and experience during the three-day event by pointing out that "our city will be profoundly impacted by the discussion generated by the geniuses and the dream circles. To have visionaries, problem solvers, dreamers, and out-of-the-box thinkers addressing issues will serve to articulate possible frameworks for addressing our future as a vital, dynamic, and multicultural city.[26]

Yet perhaps no event in Cisneros' life has so publicly challenged her cultural identity and social activism as the widely publicized controversy surrounding her choice of paint color for the house she acquired in the King William Historic District[27] in San Antonio, Texas. Originally established in the 1840s by a large German immigrant group and located south of downtown San Antonio on the east bank of the San Antonio River, King William Historic District is made up of some of the most architecturally appealing and historically significant mansions and bungalows in the city of San Antonio. The District became the first Texas neighborhood to be declared a national historic district in 1967, complete with its executive committee and eleven-member board of directors that make up the King William Association founded in the same year it was named a historic district. The King William Association is a voluntary neighborhood group elected by the active membership and designed to watch over the community's overall well-being, provide information to residents and visitors, as well as communicating ideas to city officials. The Association also hosts an annual fair as a primary fundraiser to preserve and protect the historic district and to promote the unique cultural heritage of San Antonio. In addition, the *Newsletter of the King William Association* is a monthly publication distributed from February to December to over 1,100 households that features articles on diverse neighborhood topics and issues, including an events calendar and board member profiles.

The neighborhood, rich in history and cultural diversity, has undergone significant changes since its foundation by German immigrants. Though it still houses some of San Antonio's elite and aristocratic citizens, the neighborhood has also integrated a more eclectic group of dwellers. Kathy Lowry, commenting on the social component of the District today, states that it "is renowned for its Old World charm, its stunning mix of nineteenth- and twentieth-century architectural styles, and its equally stunning stew of local personalities—prominent professionals, artists, eccentrics, wannabes, and preservationists. . . . Shaded by ancient cypress, oak, and pecan trees, this elite enclave is as different from the barrio setting and characters that Sandra Cisneros writes about as can be imagined."[28]

In 1991, Cisneros purchased a two-bedroom house on East Guenther Street in the historic district. Buying the home gave Cisneros a sense of permanence she had longed for in the most beloved and culturally relevant city in which she felt compelled to live. She describes San Antonio as "another country. This is the borderland. The beginning of Latin America. A place where two cultures collide, spark, spar, bleed and sometimes create something wonderful."[29] In 1997, Cisneros decided to paint the house in a color that would better suit its Mexican American dweller and thus chose an intense shade of purple, Sherwin Williams' Corsican Purple to be exact. Little did she realize her paint choice would cause such uproar in the neighboring community as well as in different parts of the nation through massive media coverage. Cisneros' act was seen from different perspectives either as "a cultural declaration or a political provocation, or both."[30] The house paint immediately put Cisneros at odds with the members of the city's Historic Design and Review Commission who quickly reminded Cisneros of the terms by which a house's color could be changed in the community: the color must have (1) at one time been the original color of the house, (2) appeared on at least one other house in the neighborhood, or (3) shown to have been in general use when the historic district was built.[31] Vice chairman of the historic commission, Ron Gossen, was particularly adamant about Cisneros changing her paint color, which he found "appalling" and asserted that the incident was "not about ethnicity, it's about eccentricity."[32] Cisneros accused the commission of not keeping proper historical records of the Mexican residents who formerly lived in the San Antonio town. Her response was categorically summarized in the following terms:

> The issue is bigger than my house. The issue is about historical inclusion. I want to paint my house a traditional color, but please give me a broader palette than surrey beige, sevres blue, hawthorn green, frontier days brown, and Plymouth Rock grey. . . . I thought I had painted my house a historic color. Purple is historic to us. It only goes back a thousand years or so to the pyramids. It is present in the Nahua codices, book of the Aztecs, as is turquoise, the color I used for my house trim; the former color signifying royalty, the latter, water and rain.[33]

Yet not all members of the commission disagreed with Cisneros' paint choice. Ramón Vásquez y Sánchez, board member at the time who was also responsible for overseeing public art for the city, saw the house precisely in these specific terms: as public art as well as historic. He defended Cisneros' right to choose her house's paint color by supporting her argument that "the color purple is pre-Columbian."[34] Vásquez y Sánchez further criticized the commission for using "a northeastern palette for colors" and counter-argued "what you should do is realize where you're at."[35] Others who joined in Cisneros' crusade were community members and busloads of tourists who constantly visited the historic district. Cisneros strategically placed a legal tablet attached to a clipboard on her front gate to gather the opinions of anyone who cared to remark on the controversy. She received varied remarks from people all over the country who came to see the house from as far off as Chicago and California. Some of the comments included were:

> "Beautiful house. I love the color. What's the problem?" "I love the discussion that purple has brought to the community." "I love it—they can shove it."[36]

The situation was further catapulted to national notoriety when the media began broadcasting the increasingly controversial events. When Cisneros met with the Historic Design and Review Commission on August 6, 1997, several camera crews covered the meeting for the local community, but also present were reporters from different news sources in Houston and as far as Los Angeles. Much debate ensued between Cisneros and the commission members, with no apparent agreement in sight (the members accused Cisneros of not obeying the rules of a historic district while Cisneros responded by criticizing their lack of historic specificity). Both parties were caught at an impasse when suddenly Cisneros asked, "If my house can't be purple, can I paint it another traditional Tejano color? Like the bright pink house at 312 Madison Street?"[37] To her surprise Vice President Gossen, after consulting the other members, replied, "Yes, you can." Astonished, Cisneros agreed, but not without first retaliating with the following comments: "I won't be happy until the board expands its vision to include the history and the color palette of the Tejano people. My battle won't end until that happens."[38]

And the battle certainly was far from over. Three weeks after the meeting, the local media and a CNN news crew appeared at Cisneros' home. Kathy Lowry describes the events that occurred that day:

> Seated on her lawn in a purple chair, Cisneros was dressed in a long purple dress and a purple shawl, and her pet pooch sat beside her in a purple bandanna. Just before the cameras started rolling, a Greyhound tour bus rolled up, and its driver bounded out, just inches from a "We Love Trolleys" sign. The sign, a nose-thumping gesture to Cisneros' many neighbors who are up in arms about the sight-seeing trolleys that come through King William, as well as about her purple house, was painted by Terry Ybanez [sic]. "My tourists all think your house is great!" the driver assured Cisneros. Could they hop out and take some pictures? The proud owner beamed. "Of course, if you'll all take one of these petitions"—she pointed to a ream of purple pages on a clipboard affixed to her gate—"and mail them to the mayor." The petitions were dutifully passed out. "It's not about my house," she shouted. "It's about history!"[39]

More than a year would pass with Cisneros holding her ground, rejecting the new color palettes that the board came up with as "ethnically biased color suppression."[40] While the debates raged on, San Antonio's radiant sun and smothering heat transformed the once bright Corsican Purple into a slightly lighter shade of blue, a color that both the commission members and Cisneros learned to live with. Eventually, she did paint her house pink, the color it currently holds today.

Notwithstanding the house controversy, Cisneros continued to rally and support causes that involved the Latino community. In 2000, she joined forces with other writers and social activists who rallied against capital punishment. She was one of several authors (Joan Didion, E.L. Doctorow, Elizabeth Gilbert, Adam Hochschild, Peter Maas, Michael Massing, Peter Mathiessen, Sidney Offitt, Rose Styron, William Styron, Kurt Vonnegut, among others) who joined in writing an open letter to then president Bill Clinton opposing the execution of federal prisoners. Cisneros and her fellow writers were particularly concerned over the findings of a survey conducted by the Department of Justice that revealed that three quarters of the prisoners selected for death penalty prosecution were members of ethnic or racial minorities originating in a relatively small number of states. Their most impending question was: "What can possibly account for a decision to seek the death penalty against the Hispanic defendant from Texas but not against the white defendant from New York accused of committing a crime with more egregious facts?"[41] The writers explicitly pleaded for a case involving the forthcoming execution of federal prisoner Juan Raúl Garza,[42] whose situation was an example of the larger institutionalized problem of capital punishment. Accused of drug trafficking and murder charges in 1993, Garza was convicted and sentenced to death, but the whole arrest procedure came under scrutiny when Garza's lawyers questioned the process and claimed unfair treatment. Cisneros and the other activists urged the President to change Garza's sentence to life in prison as well as impose a moratorium on federal executions, which had not been practiced since President John F. Kennedy's term in office in 1963. They specifically urged President Clinton to "pause and consider the implications of allowing any execution to proceed in the face of disturbing questions about the administration of the federal death penalty"[43] This letter joined the petitions of other concerned citizens who also opposed the death penalty and managed to postpone the execution pending further case study. Despite the fact that Garza's case was not a total victory since the execution took place the following June under President George Bush's administration, Cisneros continued to lobby against capital punishment with the hopes of one day eradicating the death penalty altogether in lieu of what she considered more humane forms of conviction that took into consideration the disadvantages in access to adequate legal representation and treatment in a court of law. In Cisneros' view, "The answer, it seems, rests primarily in the hands of the ninety-three United States attorneys across the country who wield enormous power and nearly unbridled discretion in deciding whether to prosecute a crime federally (or simply leave it to state authorities to handle), whether to charge a suspect with a potential death penalty crime, and whether to allow a defendant to plead guilty in exchange for a sentence less than death."[44]

In many ways, Cisneros' social consciousness, activism, feminism, and spirituality are inextricable from her artistic creativity. The ways in which she approaches the act of writing parallel the ways in which she goes about her daily routine—through choice and commitment—with passion and a keen awareness of her bilingual, bicultural reality. While her writing stems from the cultural/historical specificity of her Mexican heritage and her Mexican American upbringing, it rises above and beyond demarcations to that longed for and coveted territory of literary universality. In Cisneros' opinion, "to be a Chicano does not mean that one must write only about issues that Chicanos understand. Does not mean to shut out 'the others.' The element that makes it 'Chicano' is the 'awareness,' the awareness of the social condition of our fellow Chicanos and Mexicans. If we are true to ourselves how can we *not* be what we are?"[45] In this sense, Cisneros aligns herself with Philippine American writer Jessica Hagedorn whose work also proposes to subvert ethnic borders and boundaries and to "assert ourselves as artists and thinkers, to celebrate our individual histories, our rich and complicated ethnicities . . . borders be damned."[46]

Despite critical discussions on the tenets of multiculturalism, the increasing debates over literary canon formation, and the groundbreaking work of writers, scholars, and instructors in the field of multiethnic studies, there continues to be a degree of skepticism and refusal to engage in readings and/or analyses of texts written by multiethnic authors. In part, this denial can be attributed to the debate over intelligibility and meaningfulness in a written work.[47] How, then, does the conscious choice to embrace a multicultural paradigm in approaching Cisneros' and other Latinas/os' works translate into the reading of their texts? An interesting study conducted by Thomas Trzyna and Martin Abbott[48] on college students precisely addresses this concern. Issues of class, race, and gender not only came up in the works discussed in class but also in the student body and class composition itself. Trzyna's and Abbott's findings showed that students' experience in the classroom can be used to help them confront America's ethnic history, an assertion that can likewise apply to readers, both in or out of a classroom setting. Their research found that students confronted with issues of race, class, gender, social/cultural differences, and conflicting histories within the study of literature experienced sentiments similar to grief and bereavement—grief over American history, the loss of innocence, the death of students' faith in the American Dream.

Trzyna and Abbott identified several types of student reactions and behaviors that correlated to the grieving process. First, students displayed "anticipatory anxiety"[49] based on their fear of dealing with racial issues. The second reaction was denial—a sense that certain events or concepts (such as slavery and discrimination) were not as harsh as they were portrayed. Denial also came in the students' refusal to deal with certain texts' subject matter. Instead, they focused on less politically charged discussions such as literary style. Anger was also a typical student reaction often aimed at other classmates, the instructor, or controversial topics that came up in the readings. Signs of depression appeared among students who expressed feelings of general malaise or lack of energy to continue reading throughout the course.

Notwithstanding, by the end of the course, students generally expressed acceptance or approval of the course material by describing a newfound awareness and positive social action that resulted from having participated in the class. The study revealed that students exposed to ethnic studies that challenged their preconceived ideas and worldviews saw their own realities becoming more complex, inclusive, and transcultured.

Manifestations of this "grieving" process varied among students, especially those accustomed to the "old canon view"[50] of literature that might have formed part of previous literature course curricula. On the other hand, the possibility of interacting with students from different cultural backgrounds who were very much aware of the history and struggles of their people was an important aspect in the overall understanding and appreciation of the literature.[51] These students' reactions to the texts differed from students who rarely experienced any manifestations of racism or oppression. Therefore, according to Trzyna and Abbott, instructors and readers alike should adopt teaching and reading techniques that are historically comprehensive, respectful of differing opinions, and mindful of varied literary trends, styles, and traditions. By doing so, they will approach the writing with a broader scope or perspective and a richer understanding of the diversity of American literature. And this is precisely one of Cisneros' major concerns as a writer:

> I want people to recognize themselves in "the other" in my characters. I think that once you see yourself in the other, in that person who is most unlike you, then the story has done its political work. Then we cease to be "they" or "that" or "those kind," and we become humans. That recognition restores people their humanity, which is the big goal. I'm . . . neither Mexican nor completely American. From the middle, I can see the places where the two don't fit. Those interstices are always a rich place to write. When I see that a value does not quite fit in, I know that's what I have to write about.[52]

Cisneros' writing and activism continues to prosper way beyond the initial periods of her successful and award-wining career. Over the years she has become an important and influential voice both in and out of the literary word. Not only is she committed to Latino/a causes within the United States, but has also become a representative in other countries as her participation in the 1992 *Feria Internacional del Libro*[53] (International Book Fair) in Guadalajara, Mexico, clearly demonstrates. Considered one of the most prominent book festivals dating back to its foundation in 1987, the event brings together more than 1,600 publishing houses from forty different countries and over half a million visitors each year for the nine-day duration of the festival. The *FIL* has become a vital Latin American patrimony with its three constitutive components (editorial, academic, and cultural) and stands as an important nexus and meeting place for writers, academics, artists, intellectuals, and a host of other visitors interested in productive exchange of ideas and cultural debates. During the Fair, Cisneros formed part of a panel discussion, together with Rudolfo Anaya and Carlos Cumpián, to introduce their works to a predominantly Mexican

and Latin American audience. Her participation in this event marked a significant recognition of her work in the Latin American and Spanish-speaking world
of letters and publishing.

Cisneros has also been very judicious over the years when receiving requests
for anthologizing her work. She comments that "while I'm in a position to say
no to certain anthologies, I'm not always able to affect the anthology itself.
That's why I've been careful about what my being in a particular anthology
means, not just to me, but to the collective of Latino writers."[54] Often, if she is
the only Latina featured or if the title contains the word Hispanic, she chooses
not to participate as a political statement to promote change and awareness.

Cisneros continues to define herself in relation to her interaction with and
respect for the communities that have witnessed her development. She also
remains true to what she considers her works' mission:

> I have the power to make people think in a different way. It's a different way of
> defining power and it is something that I don't want to abuse or lose. I want to
> help my community. I'm a translator. I'm an amphibian. I can travel in both
> worlds. What I'm saying is very important for the Latino community, but also for
> the white community to hear. What I'm saying in my writing is that we can be
> Latino and still be American.[55]

Scott Russell Sanders points out that one of the primary reasons we enjoy
stories is "because they are a playground for language, an arena for exercising
this extraordinary power," which reminds us of "the ambiguous potency in
words, for creating or destroying, for binding or setting free."[56] This assertion
explicitly describes one of Cisneros' major accomplishments. She is an author
who continually experiments with language and narrative techniques until she
comes across modes of writing that capture and portray her experience as a
contemporary bilingual, bicultural Chicana—an experience that is far from
conventional and refuses to be encased within orthodox narrative forms or
defined by monolithic interpretations of cultural identity. This conscientious
purpose and commitment to writing may, in part, explain why critics such as
Debbie Nathan feel the need to question Cisneros' "authenticity," her cultural
background, family history, and social activism, her "biggest persona problem
. . . inventing herself as an icon."[57] Nathan's rhetoric also leads us to question
the objective of public vilification when a writer's literary works and lifestyle
are randomly or inconsistently conflated and often misinterpreted or misun-
derstood.

Through her depictions of racially mixed urban environments and cultural
and linguistic merging; her assertive search for identity and emotional release
through writing; her commitment to social causes, and her questioning of
biased gender roles, Cisneros aligns herself with other Latina writers (and
women of color writers in general) in their attempts to give voice to their
struggles as well as honor their strengths. "All the work we do as writers,"
Cisneros sustains, "is about finding balance and restoring things to balance.

You need to consider the daily choices you make to create or destroy with every single act, whether it's in words or in thoughts."[58] In accepting the challenges set forth by Cisneros' writing, the reader participates in an enriching experience of cultural awareness that will help dissipate judgments of her works as historically foreign and unapproachable. We can then join Héctor Torres in concluding that "this calls for a vast redefinition of what it means to be an American and calls into question the narrow boundaries that confine the American literary canon."[59]

Cisneros assumes the task of bearing witness to the constantly evolving Chicana/o experience and to the celebration of life as integral members of a multicultural America. The development of a *mestiza* consciousness and the important role of family and memory in the literary representation of Latina/o lives both serve to enhance the multiple subjectivities that lie at the center of her creative writing process. By inserting her languages, cultures, histories, and worldviews into the American literary scene, Sandra Cisneros provides an accurate, comprehensive, and richer portrayal of the creativity and experience of Latina women and a heightened awareness of an inclusive, multicultural American literary tradition.

Notes

INTRODUCTION

1. (Westport, CT: Praeger Press, 1997).

2. Ibid., 15.

3. Ibid., 19.

4. Ibid., 166, 167.

5. See Rudolfo Anaya and Francisco Lomelí, eds., *Aztlán: Essays on the Chicano Homeland* (Albuquerque: Univ. of New Mexico Press, 1991).

6. With the sudden influx of Chicano/a students into universities, these students rallied for schools to initiate programs relevant to their communities. They demanded ethnic studies similar to what had been implemented for African American students in colleges throughout the country. They met in the summer of 1969 at the first national Chicano Youth Conference in Denver and became an essential part of the Chicano Movement.

7. For detailed discussion on the concept of La Raza, its origins, history, and critical debates, log on to the National Council of La Raza Web site (http://www.nclr.org). Also see Emily Gantz McKay's *National Council of La Raza: First Twenty-Five Years* at http://www.nclr.org/content/publications/detail/42951, Ignacio M. García's *Chicanismo: The Forging of a Militant Ethos Among Mexican Americans* (Tucson: Univ. of Arizona Press, 1997), and also an earlier work by Stan Steiner, *La Raza: The Mexican Americans* (New York: Harper Collins, 1986), among other sources.

8. Refer to Francisco A. Rosales's *Chicano! The History of the Mexican American Civil Rights Movement* (Houston: Arte Público Press, 1996) and Marguerite V. Marin's *Social Protest in an Urban Barrio: A Study of the Chicano Movement* (Lanham, MD: Univ. Press of America, 1991), among others.

9. Norma Alarcón, "Chicana Feminism: In the Tracks of the Native Woman," *Critical Studies*, 4.3 (1990): 249.

10. *Hispanic American Literature,* Nicolas Kanellos, ed. (New York: Longman, 1995). In this play, Dolores Prida, a Cuban American playwright publishing in the 1990s, focuses on Latinas from three cultural groups: Mexican, Puerto Rican, and Cuban.

Though the guerrillera is not explicitly described as Mexican, her rhetoric and actions recall the women involved in the 1960s Chicano Movement and also can be linked to earlier participation of women in the Mexican Revolutionary War.

11. Ibid., 313.

12. See, for example, José Antonio Villarreal's *Pocho* (New York: Anchor Books, 1970; first published in 1959, Spanish translation by Doubleday Press, 1994); Luis Valdéz's *Early Works: Actos, Bernabe, and Pensamiento* Serpentino (Houston: Arte Público Press, 1990); Rodolfo González's *I am Joaquín/Yo soy Joaquín: An Epic Poem* (New York: Bantam, 1972; previously self-published in 1967); Armando Rendón's *The Chicano Manifesto* (Ollin and Associates, 1996; originally published in 1971); Rodolfo Anaya's *Bless Me, Ultima* (New York: Grand Central Publishing, 1999, Spanish translation in 1994; originally published in 1972); and Ricardo Sánchez's *Hechizospells* (Los Angeles: Univ. of California/LA Chicano Studies Series, 1976), among others.

13. Angie Chabram-Dernersesian, "I Throw Punches for My Race, But I Don't Want To Be a Man: Writing Us—Chicanos (Girl/Us)/Chicanas—Into the Movement Script," *Cultural Studies*, Lawrence Grossberg, et. al. (New York: Routledge, 1992), 82.

14. I borrow this term from Gloria Anzaldúa's seminal work: *Borderlands/La Frontera: The New Mestiza* (San Francisco: Aunt Lute Press, 1987). The concept stems from the merging of two (or more) cultures, races, languages, and worldviews to form a "third country—a border culture" that best reflects the multilayered dimensions of Latina experience and lies at the core of Latina writers' literary concerns.

15. Gloria Anzaldúa, *Borderlands/La Frontera*, 73.

16. Roberta Rubenstein, *Boundaries of the Self: Gender, Culture, Fiction* (Urbana: Univ. of Illinois Press, 1987), 5.

17. Evangelina Vigil, *Woman of Her Word: Hispanic Women Write* (Houston: Arte Público Press, 1987), 7.

18. Dale Spender, *The Writing or the Sex?* (New York: Pergamon, 1989), 113.

19. Many studies have been conducted on the exclusion of women writers from American male-oriented and male-dominated literary scenes. See, for example, Elizabeth Ammons' *Conflicting Stories: American Women Writers at the Turn Into the Twentieth Century* (New York: Oxford Univ. Press, 1991), among other sources.

20. Feroza Jussawalla and Reed Way Dasenbrock, eds., *Interviews With Writers of the Post-colonial World* (Jackson and London: Univ. Press of Mississippi, 1992), 298–299.

21. Ibid., 299.

22. Bill Ashcroft, Gareth Griffiths, and Helen Tiffin, *The Empire Writes Back* (New York: Routledge, 1989), 174.

23. Ibid., 175.

24. (Jackson and London: Univ. Press of Mississippi, 1992).

25. Writers such as Cisneros and Ana Castillo, among others, who originally published their works through Arte Público Press, Aunt Lute Books, or Third Woman Press, were now finding their way to Random House, Doubleday, Viking, and other larger presses.

26. (Boston: Kitchen Table-Women of Color Press, 1984).

27. (San Francisco: Aunt Lute Books, 1990).

28. Angie Chabram-Dernersesian, "I Throw Punches for my Race," 84.

29. (Berkeley: Third Woman Press, 1991).

30. Ibid., 1993.

31. Pilar E. Rodríguez Aranda, "On the Solitary Fate of Being Mexican, Female, Wicked and Thirty-Three: An Interview With Sandra Cisneros," *The Americas Review*, 18, no. 1 (Spring 1990): 66.

32. Gloria Anzaldúa, *Borderlands/La Frontera*, 78–80.

33. See the works of Denise Chavez, Ana Castillo, Pat Mora, Norma Cantu, Helena María Viramontes, among others.

34. Alicia Gaspar de Alba, "Literary Wetback," *Infinite Divisions: An Anthology of Chicana Literature*, Tey Diana Rebolledo and Eliana S. Rivero, eds. (Tucson: Univ. of Arizona Press, 1993), 291.

35. Irene Isabel Blea, *U.S. Chicanas and Latinas Within a Global Context: Women of Color at the Fourth World Women's Conference* (Westport, CT: Praeger Press, 1997), 15.

36. Mary Romero, Pierrette Hondagneu-Sotelo, and Vilma Ortiz, eds., *Challenging Fronteras: Structuring U.S. Latina and Latino Lives* (New York: Routledge, 1997), xv.

37. Ibid.

38. In Mary Romero, et al., *Challenging Fronteras*, 8.

39. (Nashville: Vanderbilt Univ. Press, 1997).

40. Ibid., 279.

41. Ibid., 280.

42. Pedro Cabán, "The New Synthesis of Latin American and Latino Studies" *Borderless Borders: U.S. Latinos, Latin Americans, and the Paradox of Interdependence*, Frank Bonilla, et. al. (Philadelphia: Temple Univ. Press, 1998), 212–213.

43. In the introduction to her work *On Latinidad: U.S. Latino Literature and the Construction of Identity* (Gainsville: Univ. Press of Florida, 2007), Caminero-Santangelo provides, in my opinion, the most critically comprehensive and organized discussion on the use of ethnic labels such as "Hispanic" and "Latino" and other terminology within communities of people of Latin American and Caribbean descent in the United States, which takes into account a rich array of studies conducted in the field while responsibly considering past and current debates that still abound in ethnic studies. This introduction provides a strong and informative point of reference for anyone interested in the field of Latino/a studies, literature, and ethnicity.

44. Marta Caminero-Santangelo, *On Latinidad*, 33.

45. Jussawalla and Dasenbrock, 294.

46. Marta Caminero-Santangelo, *On Latinidad*, 218–219.

47. Gloria Anzaldúa, ed., *Making Face, Making Soul/Haciendo Caras: Creative and Critical Perspectives by Feminists of Color* (San Francisco: Aunt Lute Books, 1990), xxii.

48. (Tucson: Univ. of Arizona Press, 1995), 5.

49. (Berkeley Heights, NJ: Enslow Publishers, 1998).

50. (Greensboro, NC: Morgan Reynolds Publishing, 2005).

51. Susan Snaider Lanser, *Fictions of Authority: Women Writers and Narrative Voice* (Ithaca: Cornell Univ. Press, 1992), 24.

52. (Ithaca, NY: Cornell Univ. Press, 1992).

53. (Houston: Arte Público Press, 1984; New York: Random House, 1991).

54. (New York: Knopf, 2002).

55. (New York: Random House, 1991).

56. (Bloomington, IN: Third Woman Press, 1987; revised, New York: Turtle Bay, 1992). This revised edition also includes the poems of her first poetry collection, *Bad Boys*, which appeared in 1980 by Mango Publications, but is currently out of print.

57. (New York: Knopf, 1994).
58. This film was conceived by Susan Palmer (who created the script) and produced and directed by Shelley Williams in 1995.
59. Jacqueline Stefanko, *Frontiers: A Journal of Women's Studies*, 17.2 (1996), 50.

CHAPTER ONE

1. Manifest Destiny, a term coined after the American Revolution when the first thirteen colonies gained their independence from Great Britain, called for continued territorial expansion westward and justified the annexation of new territories under religious precepts of national supremacist ideology. In other words, Americans believed it was God's will and divine providence that they conquer and settle unknown territories, regardless of anyone already established there. The belief that land was ready and available for the taking marked the early colonizers' imperialist tendencies and the beginning of continued conflicts both within these territories (especially with Native American tribes living on the land prior to European invasion) and adjacent countries such as Mexico.

2. The Treaty of Guadalupe Hidalgo, signed on February 2, 1848, put an end to the Mexican American War. Mexico ceded more than 500,000 square miles of territory to the United States extending from the Rio Grande to the Pacific Ocean. Having already gained Texas' annexation (one of the primary causes of the War), the other incorporated territories resulting from the treaty were California, Utah, Nevada, parts of Colorado, Wyoming, New Mexico, and Arizona. The Rio Grande, flowing from its source in the southern Rocky Mountains of southwestern Colorado to the Gulf of Mexico, became the new territorial boundary separating the United States from Mexico.

3. These laws also placed quotas on the number of immigrants trying to enter the United States, primarily those of European and Asian descent. The quotas did not initially affect Mexican immigrants but the immigration laws resulted in increasing impediments due to the amount of paperwork required for legal entry. For more information, see Himilce Novas, *Everything You Need to Know About Latino History* (New York: Plume, 2003).

4. Himilce Novas, *Everything You Need to Know About Latino History*, 86.

5. The Bracero Program initially ran from 1942–47 and was later reinstated in 1948–64. The program originated as a means of employment for Mexican nationals who substituted American workers sent off to World War II. The program consisted of seasonal contracts mainly for the farm and railroad industries and usually ran for one-year periods that could be renewed in some regions. Though the program represented job opportunities for millions of Mexican immigrants, the working and living conditions of those who entered the United States were less than favorable and in some cases extremely inhumane, which resulted in sociopolitical struggles and labor disputes between U.S. and Mexican government officials. Yet, at a certain point in time, *braceros* accounted for 25 percent of the workers in the farm industry of the United States. The Bracero Program ended with the introduction of machinery that substituted hand labor and the increased opposition of U.S. labor organizations that opposed the hiring of Mexican immigrants.

6. Ferozza Jusawalla and Reed Way Dasenbrock, eds., *Interviews With Writers of the Post-Colonial World* (Jackson and London: Univ. of Mississippi Press, 1992), 297.

7. Marta Satz, "Returning to One's House: An Interview with Sandra Cisneros," *Southwest Review*, 82, no. 2 (Spring 1997): 170.

8. Jussawalla and Dasenbrock, 298.

9. "Only Daughter," *Glamour* (November 1990): 256.

10. "Ghosts and Voices: Writing From Obsession," *The Americas Review*, XV, no. 1 (Spring 1987): 69.

11. Jim Sagel, "Sandra Cisneros," *Publishers Weekly* (March 29, 1991): 74.

12. "Living as a Writer: Choice and Circumstance," *Revista Mujeres*, 3, no. 2 (June 1996): 68.

13. "Notes to a Young(er) Writer," *The Americas Review*, XV, no. 1 (Spring 1987): 75.

14. Wolfgang Binder, ed. "Sandra Cisneros," *Partial Autobiographies: Interviews With Twenty Chicano Poets* (Erlangen: Verlag, Palm, & Enke, 1985), 57.

15. "Sandra Cisneros: Giving Back to the Libraries," *Schools Journal*, 119, no. 1 (January 1992): 55.

16. "Ghosts and Voices," 70.

17. "Sandra Cisneros," *Partial Autobiographies: Interviews With Twenty Chicano Poets*, 56.

18. "Ghosts and Voices," 71.

19. "Guadalupe: The Sex Goddess," *Ms*, 7, no. 1 (July 1996): 44.

20. "Only Daughter," 256.

21. "Notes to a Young(er) Writer," 74–75.

22. "Ghosts and Voices," 70.

23. Ibid., 72.

24. Eduardo Elías, "Sandra Cisneros," *Dictionary of Literary Biographies*, vol. 122, Karen Rood, ed. (Detroit: Gale Research Inc., 1992), 78.

25. "Ghosts and Voices," 72.

26. Eduardo Elías, "Sandra Cisneros," 78.

27. Renee H. Shea, "A Conversation with Sandra Cisneros" in Carol Jago's *Sandra Cisneros in the Classroom* (Urbana, IL: National Council of Teachers of English, 2002): 33.

28. (Boston: Beacon Press, 1964), Trans. María Jolas. First published under *La poétique de l'espace* (Paris: Presses Universitaires de France, 1958).

29. "Ghosts and Voices," 73.

30. "Sandra Cisneros," *Partial Autobiographies: Interviews With Twenty Chicano Poets*, 64.

31. "Ghosts and Voices," 73.

32. Ibid.

33. Caryn Merriam-Goldberg, *Sandra Cisneros: Latina Writer and Activist*. (Berkeley Heights, NJ: Enslow Publishers, 1998), 44–45.

34. (Houston: Arte Público Press, 1984; New York: Vintage, 1991). Detailed discussion of this work will follow in Chapter Two.

35. "Sandra Cisneros," *Partial Autobiographies: Interviews With Twenty Chicano Poets*, 68.

36. Sandra Cisneros, "Do You Know Me?: I Wrote The House on Mango Street," *The Americas Review*, XV, no. 1 (Spring 1987): 78.

37. Sandra Cisneros, Foreword, *Holler If You Hear Me: The Education of a Teacher and His Students*, Gregory Michie (New York: Teachers College Press, 1999), ix.

38. Ibid., ix.

39. (Berkeley: Third Woman Press, 1987; revised, New York: Random House, 1992). Detailed discussion of this poetry collection will follow in Chapter Three.

40. Robin Ganz, "Border Crossings and Beyond," *MELUS*, 19, no. 1 (1994): 25.

CHAPTER TWO

1. Detailed discussion of Cisneros' poetry will follow in Chapter 3.

2. "Do You Know Me?: I Wrote *The House on Mango Street*," *The Americas Review*, XV, no. 1 (Spring, 1987): 78.

3. Ibid., 79

4. Ibid.

5. Hereafter referred to as *Mango Street* in italics as the entire work or in regular print as the specific setting where the action takes place.

6. Carlos Queirós, "Facing Backwards," http://www.aarpsegundajuventud.org/ english/entertainment/2009-SPR/sandra_cisneros_qa.html (Accessed April 3, 2009).

7. Gary Soto, "Sandra Cisneros," *Contemporary Literary Criticism*, 69 (Detroit: Gale Research, 1992): 144.

8. Penelope Mesic, ibid., 144.

9. "Do You Know Me?" 78.

10. Alvina Quintana, "Borders be Damned: Creolizing Literary Relations," *Cultural Studies*, 13, no. 2 (1999): 359.

11. Annie Eysturoy, *Daughters of Self-Creation: The Contemporary Chicana Novel* (Albuquerque: Univ. of New Mexico Press, 1996), 89.

12. While First Wave Feminism (late 1800s to early 1900s) focused on important issues such as woman's suffrage and birth control rights, Second Wave Feminism (1960–1982) pushed for greater equality in other areas such as education, the workplace, and the home. For more information, see Sara Evans and Stephanie Gilmore, *Feminist Coalitions: Historical Perspectives on Second-Wave Feminism in the United States* (Urbana-Champaign: Univ. of Illinois Press, 2008) and Linda Nicholson's edition of *The Second Wave: A Reader in Feminist Theory* (New York: Routledge, 1997), among other sources.

13. Some of these accomplishments include The Commission on the Status of Women under the John F. Kennedy administration; the publication of Betty Friedan's groundbreaking work, *The Feminine Mystique*; Title VII of the Civil Rights Act, which prohibited employment discrimination based on sex, race, religion, and national origin; Title IX, which forbade discrimination in the field of education; the foundation of the National Organization for Women (NOW); the decision to legalize abortion and recognize women's rights regarding reproduction (Roe vs. Wade) consistent with the right to privacy under the 14th Amendment to the U. S. Constitution; among others.

14. Pilar E. Rodriguez Aranda, "On the Solitary Fate of Being Mexican, Female, Wicked, and Thirty-three: An Interview With Sandra Cisneros," *The Americas Review*, 9, no.1 (Spring 1990): 69.

15. Ibid.

16. Portions of this discussion were originally published as part of a longer comparative study I conducted on the works of Sandra Cisneros and Ana Castillo. The article, "Breaking the Rules: Innovation and Narrative Strategies in Sandra Cisneros's *The House*

on Mango Street and Ana Castillo's *The Mixquiahuala Letters*" appeared in *Ethnic Studies Review*, 26, no. 1 (2003): 108–120.

17. *The House on Mango Street* (New York: Random House, 1989), 11. All subsequent quotes referred to by page number.

18. Julian Olivares, "Entering *The House on Mango Street*," *Teaching American Ethnic Literatures*, John R. Maitano and David R. Peck, eds. (Albuquerque: Univ. of New Mexico Press, 1996), 213.

19. Renee H. Shea, "A Conversation with Sandra Cisneros" in Carol Jago's *Sandra Cisneros in the Classroom: "Don't Forget to Reach"* (Urbana, IL: National Council of Teachers of English, 2002): 34–35.

20. Maxine Hong Kingston, *The Woman Warrior* (New York: Vintage, 1989).

21. Alvina Quintana, "Borders Be Damned," 363–362.

22. For more information on Third Wave Feminism, see Stacy Gillis's, Gillian Howie's, and Rebecca Munford's *Third Wave Feminism: A Critical Exploration* (New York: Palgrave Macmillan, 2007) and Astrid Henry's *Not My Mother's Sister: Generational Conflict and Third-Wave Feminism* (Bloomington: Indiana Univ. Press, 2004), among other sources.

23. Bonnie TuSmith, *All My Relatives: Community in Contemporary Ethnic American Literature* (Ann Arbor: Univ. of Michigan Press, 1994), 161.

24. Feroza Jussawalla and Reed Way Dasenbrock, *Interviews With Writers of the Post-Colonial World* (Jackson and London: Univ. Press of Mississippi, 1992), 302.

25. Jean Wyatt, "On Not Being La Malinche: Border Negotiations of Gender in the Works of Sandra Cisneros," *Studies in Women's Literature*, 14, no. 2 (1995): 266.

26. Bonnie TuSmith, *All My Relatives*, 164.

27. In a review of *The House on Mango Street* in the *Austin Chronicle* (10 August 1984), Juan Rodríguez comments: "That Esperanza chooses to leave Mango St., chooses to move away from her social/cultural base to become more 'Anglicized,' more individualistic; that she chooses to move from the real to the fantasy plane of the world as the only means of accepting and surviving the limited and limiting social conditions of her barrio becomes problematic to the more serious reader."

28. Caryn Mirriam-Goldberg, *Sandra Cisneros: Latina Writer and Activist* (Berkeley Heights, NJ: Enslow Publishers, 1998), 55.

29. "Ghosts and Voices: Writing From Obsession," *The Americas Review*, XV, no. 1 (Spring 1987): 73.

30. *The Woman Warrior: Memoirs of a Childhood Among Ghosts* (New York: Vintage, 1989); *Beloved* (New York: Plume, 1988).

31. See Toni Morrison's "Unspeakable Things Unspoken: The Afro-American Presence in American Literature," *Michigan Quarterly Review*, 28, no. 1 (Winter, 1989): 1–34.

32. Ramola D., "An Interview With Sandra Cisneros," *The Writer's Chronicle*, 38, no. 6 (May 2006): 4.

33. Gayle Elliott, "An Interview With Sandra Cisneros," *The Missouri Review*, 25, no. 1 (2002): 109.

34. Elsa Saeta, "An Interview with Ana Castillo," *MELUS*, 22, no. 3 (1997): 140.

35. Information on the Before Columbus American Book Award obtained from the following Web site: http://www.ankn.uaf.edu/IEW/BeforeColumbus/index2002.html.

36. Cisneros originally began to write these poems while she attended the University of Iowa Writers Workshop. She continued to write both during her sojourns in Europe and upon her return to the United States and these are the poems that would later form part of this publication. I will provide further analysis of this work in Chapter 3.

37. Jussawalla and Dasenbrock, 298.

38. Sandra Cisneros, "Who Wants Stories Now?" *New York Times* (March 14, 1993): 17.

39. A copy of Jasna's letter appeared in *The New York Times* as "Letter From Sarajevo" on April 9, 1993, p. A12.

40. "Who Wants Stories Now?" 17.

41. Jussawalla and Dasenbrock, 295–296.

42. Sandra Cisneros, "The Tejano Soul of San Antonio," *New York Times Magazine* (May 17, 1992): 24.

43. Ibid., 42.

44. Jussawalla and Dasenbrock, 299.

45. Ibid.

46. Information on the Dobie Paisano Award obtained from the following Web site: http://www.utexas.edu/ogs/Paisano.

47. Sandra Cisneros, "The Tejano Soul of San Antonio," 42.

48. "Do You Know Me?" 77.

49. Pilar E. Rodriguez Aranda, "On the Solitary Fate...," 77.

50. Raul Niño, "The Booklist Interview, Sandra Cisneros," *Booklist* (September 1, 1993): 36.

51. "Ghosts and Voices," 73.

52. Cathy Cockrell, "A Labor of Love, A Publishing Marathon," *Berkeleyan Home Search Archive*, http://www.berkeley.edu/news/berkeleyan/1999/0512/alarcon.html (accessed October 18, 2007).

53. Pilar E. Rodriguez Aranda, "On the Solitary Fate...," 71.

54. Ibid., 72.

55. Marta Satz, "Returning to One's House: An Interview with Sandra Cisneros," *Southwest Review*, 82, no. 2 (Spring 1997): 182.

56. Jussawalla and Dasenbrock, 300–301.

57. (New York: Vintage Books/Random House, 1991), herein after referred to as *Woman Hollering Creek*.

58. Harryette Mullen, "A Silence Between Us Like a Language: The Untranslatability of Experience in Sandra Cisneros's *Woman Hollering Creek*, *MELUS*, 21, no 2 (Summer 1996): 8.

59. *Woman Hollering Creek*, 35; subsequent quotes referred to by page number.

60. See, for example, Tey Diana Rebolledo's *Women Singing in the Snow: A Cultural Analysis of Chicana Literature* (Tucson: Univ. of Arizona Press, 1995) and Phillipa Kafka's *(Out)Classed Women: Contemporary Chicana Writers on Inequitable Gender Power Relations* (Westport, CT: Greenwood Press, 2000).

61. Virginia Brackett, *A Home in the Heart: The Story of Sandra Cisneros* (Greensboro, NC: Morgan Reynolds Publishing, 2005): 71.

62. Jussawalla and Dasenbrock, 300.

63. Erlinda González-Berry, review of *Woman Hollering Creek and Other Stories*, by Sandra Cisneros, *The Americas Review* 20, no.1 (Spring 1991): 84–85.

64. Harryette Mullen, "A Silence Between Us Like a Language," 4.

65. Reed Way Dasenbrock, "Intelligibility and Meaningfulness in Multicultural Literature in English," *PMLA*, 102, no. 1 (January 1987): 14–15.

66. Ibid., 18.

67. Ibid.

68. Jussawalla and Dasenbrock, 290.

69. Information on the Lannan award obtained from the following Web site: http://www.lannan.org/lf/programs/lit.

70. Information on the Edith Anisfield-Wolf Book Award obtained from the following Web site: http/:www.anisfield-wolf.org/aboutus/default.aspz?id=522.

71. Jim Sagel, "Sandra Cisneros," *Publisher's Weekly* (March 29, 1991): 74.

72. "House on Mango Street: A Novel Hits the Hustings," http://www.labloga.blogaspot.com/2005/03/house-on-mango-street-novel-hits.html (accessed November 1, 2007).

73. Functioning as the cultural arm for the United Farm Workers led by Cesar Chavez, *Teatro Campesino* originated with short sketches (*actos*) often performed by the farm workers themselves, first for entertainment then as a means of fundraising for the striking workers. Their subject matter, however, was not only limited to the fields but also included protests against racism, the Vietnam War, and educational inequality. The focus on indigenous roots and cultural pride specifically connected to Mexican idiosyncrasy made the sketches particularly appealing and meaningful. For more information on *Teatro Campesino*, see http://www.teatrocampesino.com.

74. A variety of traditions merged in the early performances of *Teatro Campesino* sketches that often involved Spanish religious dramas, Mexican folk humor, and Aztec and Maya sacred ritual dramas.

CHAPTER THREE

1. I borrow the first half of this chapter title from Gloria Anzaldúa's *Borderlands/La Frontera: The New Mestiza* in which she relates the power of the word with the goddess Coatlicue and Latinas overcoming a tradition of silence. See Chapters 3 to 5 in Anzaldúa's work.

2. Victor Hernández Cruz, "Mountains in the North: Hispanic Writing in the U.S.A," *The Americas Review*, 14, no. 3–4 (Fall–Winter, 1986): 110.

3. By diasporic Puerto Rican, I refer to the writers of Puerto Rican descent who, like Victor Hernández Cruz, have made the United States (among other places) their home and who publish mainly in English, though often reverting to Spanish and/or Spanglish in their writing. Because these writers are for the most part bilingual and bicultural, they share common experiences and thematic concerns with their fellow Chicano/a writers. For more information on this subject, see Juan Bruce-Novoa's "A Case of Identity: What's in a Name? Chicanos and Riqueños," in *Retrospace: Collected Essays on Chicano Literature* (Houston: Arte Público Press, 1990): 33–40, and Edna Acosta-Belén, et al. *"Adiós, Borinquen Querida": The Puerto Rican Diaspora, Its History, and Contributions* (Albany: CELAC, 1990).

4. Victor Hernández Cruz, "Mountains in the North," 111–112, 114.

5. Pilar E. Rodríguez Aranda, "On the Solitary Fate of Being Mexican, Female, Wicked, and Thirty-three: An Interview with Writer Sandra Cisneros," *The Americas Review*, 18, no. 1 (1990): 75.

6. Wolfgang Binder, ed., "Sandra Cisneros," *Partial Autobiographies: Interviews With Twenty Chicano Poets* (Erlangen: Verlag, Palm & Enke, 1985): 66–67.

7. Ramola D., "An Interview with Sandra Cisneros," *The Writer's Chronicle*, 38, no. 6 (Summer 2006): 6.

8. Sandra Cisneros, *The House on Mango Street* (New York: Random House, 1989) and *Woman Hollering Creek and Other Stories* (New York: Random House, 1991).

9. "Sandra Cisneros," *Partial Autobiographies: Interviews With Twenty Chicano Poets* 71–72.

10. Ellen McCracken, "Sandra Cisneros (1954–)," *Latino and Latina Writers*, Alan West-Duran, et al. (New York: Thomson/Gale, 2004): 234.

11. Herein after referred to as *Wicked Ways*. All quotes from the 1992 edition.

12. Ramola D., "Interview with Sandra Cisneros," 9.

13. Ibid.

14. Pilar E. Rodríguez Aranda, "On the Solitary Fate . . . .," 74.

15. Martha Satz, "Returning to One's House: An Interview with Sandra Cisneros." *Southwest Review*, 82, no. 2 (Spring 1997): 174.

16. Pilar E. Rodríguez Aranda, "On the Solitary Fate . . . .," 67.

17. Ibid., 68.

18. Ibid., 69.

19. Ibid., 75.

20. Sandra Cisneros, "Guadalupe the Sex Goddess: Unearthing the Racy Past of Mexico's Most Famous Virgin," *Ms.*, VII, no. 1 (July–August 1996): 45.

21. Ibid.

22. Ibid., 46.

23. Sandra Cisneros, *My Wicked Wicked Ways* (New York: Random House, 1992): 26. Quotes from the text herein after referred to by page number.

24. Hector Torres, "Sandra Cisneros: Two Interviews," *Conversations with Contemporary Chicana and Chicano Writers* (Albuquerque: Univ. of New Mexico Press, 2007): 215–216.

25. Tey Diana Rebolledo, *Woman Singing in the Snow: A Cultural Analysis of Chicana Literature* (Tucson: Univ. of Arizona Press, 1995): 192.

26. Ibid., 193.

27. Adriana Estill, "Building the Chicana Body in Sandra Cisneros' *My Wicked Wicked Ways*," *Rocky Mountain Review of Language and Literature*, 56, no. 2 (2002): 34.

28. Ibid., 38.

29. Pilar E. Rodríguez Aranda, "On the Solitary Fate...", 75.

30. (New York: Random House, 1994).

31. Martha Satz, "Returning to One's House: An Interview with Sandra Cisneros," *Southwest Review*, 82, no. 2 (Spring 1997): 172.

32. Ibid., 174.

33. Pilar E. Rodríguez Aranda, "On the Solitary Fate...", 79.

34. Hector Torres, "Sandra Cisneros: Two Interviews," 207.

35. Xochitl Estrada Shuru. *The Poetics of Hysteria in Chicana Writing: Sandra Cisneros, Margarita Cota-Cárdenas, Pat Mora, and Bernice Zamora.* PhD diss., Univ. of New Mexico Press, 2000, 114.

36. Barbara Hoffert, "Cisneros, Sandra, *Loose Woman*: Poems," *Library Journal* (May 15, 1994): 76.

37. Sandra Cisneros, *Loose Woman* (New York: Random House, 1994): 6. Quotes from the text herein after referred to by page number.

38. Ellen McCracken, "Sandra Cisneros (1954–)," 236.

39. See Chapter 2 for more details on Cisneros' relationship to Jasna.

40. Gayle Elliott, "An Interview With Sandra Cisneros," *The Missouri Review*, 25, no. 1: 105.

41. Ibid., 106.

42. Martha Satz, "Returning to One's House: An Interview with Sandra Cisneros," 175.

43. Ellen McCracken, "Sandra Cisneros (1954–)," 236.

44. Martha Satz, "Returning to One's House: An Interview with Sandra Cisneros," 172.

CHAPTER FOUR

1. To be able to transcend in history so that our deeds are remembered, someone needs to mention our name.

2. Information on the U.S.–Mexico border obtained form the following Web sites: http://www.google.com.pr/search?hl=es&q=U.S.-Mexico+Border&btnG=Buscar+con+Google&lr= and http://en.wikipedia.org/wiki/United_States%E2%80%93Mexico_barrier (accessed January 7, 2009).

3. The Secure Fence Act was a multibillion dollar initiative for building a fence that separated the U.S.–Mexico border to prevent illegal entry of undocumented immigrants and to provide security from potential terrorists using the border to enter the United States. Huge controversy surrounds the Act since the proposed fence will eventually cover less than half of the actual border and will literally run through the middle of individually owned properties and public buildings while leaving other territories without surveillance. Many people question whether the fence serves its purpose or whether it is just another waste of financial and human resources. For more information concerning this topic, see http://www.pbs.org/now/shows/432/.

4. The U.S. Border Patrol, whose initial efforts date as far back as the early 1900s, is a federal law enforcement agency within the Department of Homeland Security. Its primary responsibility is the arrest of illegal immigrants, terrorists, or individuals involved in illegal drug trading who try to enter the United States. Several articles, books, and films, however, have consistently denounced the systematic abuse and human rights violations perpetrated by Border Patrol agents. For a list of such sources and additional information on this subject, see http://en.wikipedia.org/wiki/United_States_Border_Patrol, among others.

5. The following statistical information on Mexican immigration, along with various links to sources that discuss U.S.–Mexico relations and border crossings in detail, can be found at http://www.migrationinformation.org/Feature/display.cfm?id=407.

6. See http://www.globalsecurity.org/security/systems/mexico-wall.htm for more information.

7. Esmeralda Santiago's memoir *When I Was Puerto Rican* and its translation *Cuando era puertorriqueña* also benefited from this publishing and sales strategy though the translation was published a year after the original English version.

8. Arianne Schultheis, "Sandra Cisneros Plays with the Notion of Boundaries," *New University Online*, http://www.newuniversity.org/plain_article.php?id=1629 (accessed February 19, 2008).

9. Ann Burns, "Caramelo," *Library Journal*, 128, no. 7 (April 15, 2003): 146.

10. Ibid.

11. Keir Graff, "Caramelo," *Audio for Adults* (March 1, 2003): 1213.

12. Ibid.

13. "Caramelo (Book)," *Publishers Weekly*, 250, no.9 (March 3, 2003).

14. Ray Suárez, "Conversation: Cisneros," *Online NewsHour*, http://www.pbs.org/newhour/conversation/july-dec02/cisneros_10-15.html (accessed February 19, 2008).

15. Ed Morales, "Imaginary Homeland, Interview: Sandra Cisneros," *Críticas* (September/October 2002): 29.

16. At the beginning of the novel, Cisneros includes a disclaimer stating that "these stories are nothing but stories, bits of string, odds and ends found here and there, embroidered together to make something new. I have invented what I do not know and exaggerated what I do know to continue the family tradition of telling healthy lies. If, in the course of my inventing, I have accidentally stumbled on the truth, *perdónenme*."

17. Ed Morales, "Imaginary Homeland, Interview: Sandra Cisneros," 30.

18. Ilan Stavans, "Familia Faces: *Caramelo*," *Nation*, 276, no. 5 (February 10, 2003), http://www.thenation.com/docprem.mhtml?!=20030210&s=stavans (accessed Febrary 19, 2008).

19. Ibid.

20. Ibid.

21. Ibid.

22. Ray Suárez, "Conversation: Cisneros," *Online NewsHour*, http://www.pbs.org/newhour/conversation/july-dec02/cisneros_10-15.html (accessed February 19, 2008).

23. Ramola D., "An Interview With Sandra Cisneros," *The Writer's Chronicle*, (May 2006): 5.

24. This statement comes up in a telephone interview with María Newman, excerpts of which Newman later published in an article titled "Sandra Cisneros: Her New Book, Her New Look" for *Hispanic Journal*. Though Cisneros refers to this girl as inspiration for the novel's title, I will later discuss how the term acquires other tangible as well as metaphorical significances.

25. Bill Johnson González, "The Politics of Translation in Sandra Cisneros's *Caramelo*," *Differences: A Journal of Feminist Cultural Studies*, 17, no. 3 (2006): 4.

26. Gabriella Gutiérrez y Muhs, "Sandra Cisneros and Her Trade of the Free Word," *Rocky Mountain Review* (Fall 2006): 27.

27. Ibid.

28. Sandra Cisneros, *Caramelo or Puro Cuento* (New York: Knopf, 2002): 4. All subsequent quotes from this work will be referred to by page number.

29. Robert Birnbaum, "Sandra Cisneros," *Identity Theory*, http:// www.identitytheory.com/printme/cisnerosprint.html (accessed February 19, 2008).

30. Ed Morales, "Imaginary Homeland, Interview: Sandra Cisneros," 32.

31. Robert Birnbaum, "Sandra Cisneros," *Identity Theory*, http:// www.identity theory.com/printme/cisnerosprint.html (accessed February 19, 2008).

32. Gayle Elliott, "An Interview With Sandra Cisneros," *The Missouri Review*, 25, no. 1 (2002): 102.

33. Ibid., 104–105.

34. Bill Johnson González, "The Politics of Translation in Sandra Cisneros's *Caramelo*," 14.

35. Gloria Anzaldúa, *Borderlands/ La Frontera: The New Mestiza* (San Francisco, Aunt Lute Books, 1987): 79.

36. Gabriella Gutiérrez y Muhs, "Sandra Cisneros and Her Trade of the Free Word," 28–29.

37. Ibid., 33.

38. Ellen McCracken, "Sandra Cisneros (1954–)," *Latino and Latina Writers*, ed. Alan West-Duran (New York: Thomson/Gale, 2004): 244.

39. Marta Satz, "Returning to One's House: An Interview with Sandra Cisneros," *Southwest Review*, 82., no. 2 (Spring 1997): 184.

40. Information on the MacArthur Foundation obtained from the following Web site: http://www.macfound.org.

41. *Latina Self-Portraits: Interviews with Contemporary Women Writers* (Albuquerque: Univ. of New Mexico Press, 2000): 45–57.

42. Ibid., 53–54.

43. Jen Buchendorff, "Father's death opened new insights for 'Caramelo' author Sandra Cisneros," *The Seattle Times* (October 21, 2003), http:// community.seattle times.nwsource.com/archive/?date=20031021&slug=cisneros21.

44. Robert Birnbaum, "Sandra Cisneros," *Identity Theory*, http:// www.identity theory.com/printme/cisnerosprint.html (accessed February 19, 2008).

45. Virginia Brackett, *A Home in the Heart: The Story of Sandra Cisneros* (Greensboro, NC: Morgan, Reynolds, 2005): 115.

CHAPTER FIVE

1. I borrow this term from anthropologist and social scientist Jorge Duany's work *The Puerto Rican Nation on the Move*, a term that he describes as "a transient and pendulous flow, rather than as a permanent, irrevocable, one-way relocation of people" that might serve as "an apt metaphor for the fluid and hybrid identities" (3) of those involved in the movement. Duany concludes, therefore, that "none of the traditional criteria for nation-hood—a shared territory, language, economy, citizenship, or sovereignty—are fixed and immutable . . . but are subject to constant fluctuations and intense debate, even though the sense of people-hood has proven remarkably resilient throughout" (4). Though Duany applies this argument mainly to Puerto Ricans who migrate to the United States, I find similar parallels and points of convergence with the Mexican American community.

2. In *Borderlands/La Frontera*, Gloria Anzaldúa defines this term as "an act of kneading, of uniting and joining" that "participates in the creation of yet another cul-ture, a new story to explain the world and our participation in it, a new value system with images and symbols that connect us to each other and to the planet" (81). In other words, a combination of cultures, languages, and worldviews that characterize the Latino/a population in the United States.

3. Wolfgang Binder, ed., *Partial Autobiographies: Interviews With Twenty Chicano Poets* (Erlangen: Verlag, Palm & Enke, 1985): 67–68.

4. Ibid., 69.

5. Information on the Women Make Movies series obtained from the following Web site: http://www.wmm.com/about/general_info.shtml.

6. All quotes and references are directly transcribed from the film version.

7. *The Dessert Is No Lady: Landscapes in Women's Writing and Art*, Women Make Movies series.

8. Ibid.

9. Jim Sagel, "Sandra Cisneros," *Publishers Weekly* (March 29, 1991): 75.

10. Jeff Thomson, "'What Is Called Heaven': Identity in Sandra Cisneros's Woman Hollering Creek," *Studies in Short Fiction*, 33, no. 3 (Summer 1994): 415.

11. *The Dessert Is No Lady: Landscapes in Women's Writing and Art*, Women Make Movies series.

12. Information on the Macondo Workshop obtained from the following Web site: http://www.macondoworkshop.org/html.

13. Quoted in Vicente Lozano's article "The Macondo Workshop: Latino Writers Come Home to San Antonio," *Poets and Writers* (March/April 2007): 70.

14. Vicente Lozano, "The Macondo Workshop," 71, 73.

15. Ramola D., "An Interview With Sandra Cisneros," *The Writer's Chronicle*, 38, no. 6 (May 2006): 8.

16. Information on the Esperanza Peace and Justice Center obtained from the following Web site: http://www.esperanzacenter.org.

17. Vicente Lozano, "The Macondo Workshop," 74.

18. Information on the Elvira Cordero Cisneros Award obtained from the following Web site: http://sandracisneros.com/2008-02-14_elvira_award.php.

19. Ibid.

20. http:// www.sandracisneros.com/foundation.php

21. Sandra Cisneros, http://www.macondofoundation.org/programs_casa.html (accessed July 30, 2008).

22. http://www.sandracisneros.com/macarturos.php.

23. Ibid.

24. http://macarturos.blogspot.com (accessed July 21, 2008).

25. "Los MacArturos tackling major problems," http://www.sanantonio.com/news/MYSA100507_03B_MacArturos_388a039_html5135.html (accessed July 21, 2008).

26. Ibid.

27. Information on the King William district obtained from the following Web sites: http://www.accd.edu/sac/english/mcquien/htmlfils/kingwill.htm and http://www.informationsanantonio.com/kingwilliam.htm.

28. Kathy Lowry, "The Purple Passion of Sandra Cisneros," *Texas Monthly*, 25, no. 10 (October 1997): 149.

29. Sandra Cisneros, "The Tejano Soul of San Antonio," *New York Times* (May 17, 1992): 24.

30. Kathy Lowry, "The Purple Passion of Sandra Cisneros," 149.

31. Ibid., 150.

32. Sara Rimer, "Novelist's Purple Palette Is Not to Everyone's Taste," *New York Times* (July 13, 1998), http://www.nytimes.com/ref/membercenter/nytarchive.html (accessed 20 April 2008).

33. http://www.informationsanantonio.com/kingwilliam.htm.

34. Sara Rimer, "Novelist's Purple Palette Is Not to Everyone's Taste," *New York Times* (July 13, 1998), http://www.nytimes.com/ref/membercenter/nytarchive.html (accessed 20 April 2008).

35. Ibid.

36. Ibid.

37. Kathy Lowry, "The Purple Passion of Sandra Cisneros," 150.

38. Ibid.

39. Ibid.

40. Ibid.

41. "An Open letter to the President," *The New York Review of Books*, 47, no.20 (December 21, 2000), http://www.nybooks.com/articles/13937 (accessed 30 April 2008).

42. http://ccadp.org/juanraulgarza.htm.

43. Ibid.

44. Ibid.

45. Wolfgang Binder, ed., *Partial Autobiographies: Interviews With Twenty Chicano Poets*, 68–69.

46. Jessica Hagedorn, Introduction, *Danger and Beauty* (San Francisco: City Lights Books, 2002): vii.

47. In his article "Intelligibility and Meaningfulness in Multicultural Literature in English" (PMLA 1987), Reed Way Dasenbrock objects to universalist critics who argue that barriers to readily intelligible reading (such as the use of other languages, idiomatic phrases, and cultural codes within an English language narration) produce flawed texts. Dasenbrock states that "the reader who is interested in a work should expect to do some work to appreciate it." It is, therefore, up to the reader to acquire the necessary knowledge to obtain a productive reading experience from the text. For further discussion, see Chapter 2.

48. See "Grieving in the Ethnic Literature Classroom," *College Literature*, 18, no. 3 (1991): 1–14.

49. Ibid., 3.

50. See Jerry Martin's "The Core Curriculum and the Canon: the Struggle and the Debate" in *The Core and the Canon: National Debate,* L. Robert Stevens, et al. (Houston: Univ. of North Texas Press, 1993, 3–9). Martin describes the "old canon view" as one that only considers a fixed body of "Great Books" that rarely changes over time because they meet standards of excellence and truth. These standards, however, have been the topic of much critical debate both in this volume and other works. See, for example, A. LaVonne Brown Ruoff and Jerry W. Ward, eds. *Redefining American Literary History* (New York: MLA, 1990), Paul Lauter's *Canons and Contexts* (New York: Oxford Univ. Press, 1991), and John Guillory's *Cultural Capital: The Problem of Literary Canon Formation* (Chicago: Univ. of Chicago Press, 1995), for further discussion.

51. Many of these students may be second- or third-generation immigrant descendents familiar with their cultural and family histories and may have witnessed struggles for social justice and equality in the United States. See, for example, Asunción Horno-Delgado's *Breaking Boundaries: Latina Writing and Critical Readings* (Amherst: Univ. of Massachusetts Press, 1989).

52. Renee H. Shea, "A Conversation with Sandra Cisneros" in Carol Jago's *Sandra Cisneros in the Classroom: "Don't Forget to Reach,"* (Urbana, IL: National Council of Teachers of English, 2002): 35–36.

53. Information on the *Feria Internacional del Libro* obtained from the following Web site: http://www.fil.com.mx/info/info_hist.asp.

54. Raúl Niño, "The Booklist Interview, Sandra Cisneros," *Booklist* (September 1, 1993): 37.

55. Mary B. W. Tabor, "A Solo Traveler in Two Worlds," *New York Times* (January 7, 1993): C1, C10.

56. Scott Russell Sanders, "The Most Human Art: Ten Reasons Why We'll Always Need a Good Story," *Georgia Review* (September/October 1997): 55.

57. Debbie Nathan, "Can Sandra Survive San Antonio?—Can San Antonio Survive Her?" *San Antonio Current* (October, 1999): 18, 21.

58. Carlos Queirós, "Facing Backwards" http://www.aarpsegundajuventud.org/english/entertainment/2009-SPR/sandra_cisneros_qa.html (Accessed April 3, 2009).

59. Héctor Torres, "Story, Telling, Voice: Narrative Authority in Ana Castillo's *The Mixquiahuala Letters*," *Chicana (W)rites: On Word and Film* (Ann Arbor: Univ. of Michigan Press, 1994), 143.

Bibliography

Alarcón, Norma. "Chicana Feminism: In the Tracks of the Native Woman." *Critical Studies*. 4, no. 3 (1990): 248–256.

Alarcón, Norma, Cherríe Moraga, and Ana Castillo, eds. *The Sexuality of Latinas*. Boston: Kitchen Table, Women of Color Press, 1984.

Ammons, Elizabeth. *Conflicting Stories: American Women Writers at the Turn into the Twentieth Century*. New York: Oxford Univ. Press, 1991.

Anaya, Rudolfo. *Bless Me, Ultima*. New York: Grand Central Publishing, 1999; Spanish translation, 1994; originally published in 1972.

Anaya, Rudolfo, and Francisco Lomelí, eds. *Aztlán: Essays on the Chicano Homeland*. Albuquerque: Univ. of New Mexico Press, 1991.

Anzaldúa, Gloria. *Borderlands/La Frontera: The New Mestiza*. San Francisco: Aunt Lute Press, 1987.

———, ed. *Making Face, Making Soul/Haciendo Caras: Creative and Critical Perspectives by Feminists of Color*. San Francisco: Aunt Lute Press, 1990.

Ashcroft, Bill, Gareth Griffiths, and Helen Tiffin. *The Empire Writes Back*. New York: Routledge, 1989.

Bachelard, Gaston. *The Poetics of Space*. Trans. María Jolas. Boston: Beacon Press, 1964.

Binder, Wolfgang, ed. "Sandra Cisneros." *Partial Autobiographies: Interviews with Twenty Chicano Poets*. Erlangen: Verlag, Palm & Enke, 1985.

Blea, Irene Isabel. *U.S. Chicanas and Latinas Within a Global Context: Women of Color at the Fourth World Women's Conference*. Westport, CT: Praeger Press, 1997.

Brackett, Virginia. *A Home in the Heart: The Story of Sandra Cisneros*. Greensboro, NC: Morgan Reynolds Publishing, 2005.

Birnbaum, Robert. "Sandra Cisneros." *Identity Theory*. http://www.identitytheory.com/printme/cisnerosprint.html (Accessed February 19, 2008).

Buchendorff, Jen. "Father's Death Opened New Insights for 'Caramelo' Author Sandra Cisneros." *The Seattle Times* (October 21, 2003), http//community.seattletimes.nwsource.com/archive/?date=20031021&slug=cisne ros21 (Accessed May 13, 2008).

Burns, Ann. "Caramelo." *Library Journal* 128, no. 7 (April 15, 2003): 146.

Cabán, Pedro. "The New Synthesis of Latin American and Latino Studies." *Borderless Borders: U.S. Latinos, Latin Americans, and the Paradox of Interdependence*. Frank Bonilla, et al., eds. Philadelphia: Temple Univ. Press, 1998, 212–213.

Caminero-Santangelo, Marta. *On Latinidad: U.S. Latino Literature and the Construction of Ethnicity*. Gainsville: Univ. Press of Florida, 2007.

Chabram-Dernesisian, Angie. "I Throw Punches for My Race, but I Don't Want To Be a Man: Writing Us—Chica-nos (Girl/Us)/Chicanas—Into the Movement Script." *Cultural Studies*, Lawrence Grossberg, et al., eds. New York: Routledge, 1992, 81–95.

Cisneros, Sandra. *Caramelo, O Puro Cuento*. New York: Knopf, 2002.

———. *Loose Woman*. New York: Knopf, 1994.

———. *My Wicked Wicked Ways*. Berkeley: Third Woman Press, 1987; revised, New York: Random House, 1992.

———. *Woman Hollering Creek and Other Stories*. Berkeley: Third Woman Press, 1987; New York: Random House, 1991.

———. *The House on Mango Street*. Houston: Arte Público Press, 1984; New York: Vintage, 1991.

Cisneros, Sandra, et al. "An Open letter to the President." *The New York Review of Books* 47, no. 20 (December 21, 2000), http://www.nybooks.com/articles/13937 (Accessed May 13, 2008).

Cisneros, Sandra. Foreword. *Holler If You Hear Me: The Education of a Teacher and His Students*. Gregory Michie, New York: Teachers College Press, 1999, ix–xii.

———. "Guadalupe the Sex Goddess: Unearthing the Racy Past of Mexico's Most Famous Virgin." *Ms.* VII, no. 1 (July–August 1996): 43–46.

———. "Sandra Cisneros: Giving Back to the Libraries." *Schools Journal.* 119, no. 1 (January 1992): 55.

———. "The Tejano Soul of San Antonio." *New York Times Magazine* (May 17, 1992): 24–42.

———. "Only Daughter." *Glamour* (November 1990): 256–257.

———. "Ghosts and Voices: Writing From Obsession." *The Americas Review* XV, no. 2 (1987): 69–73.

———. "Notes to a Young Writer." *The Americas Review* XV, no. 2 (1987): 74–76.

———. "Do You Know Me?: I Wrote *The House on Mango Street*." *The Americas Review* XV, no. 2 (1987): 77–79.

———. "Living as a Writer: Choice and Circumstance." *Revista Mujeres* 3, no. 2 (1986): 68–72.

Cockrell, Cathy. "A Labor of Love, A Publishing Marathon." *Berkeleyan Home Search Archive*, http://www.berkeley.edu/news/berkeleyan/1999/0512/alarcon.html (Accessed October 18, 2007).

D., Ramola. "An Interview with Sandra Cisneros." *The Writer's Chronicle* 38, no. 6 (May 2006): 4–12.

Dasenbrock, Reed Way. "Intelligibility and Meaningfulness in Multicultural Literature in English." *PMLA* 102, no. 1 (January 1987): 10–18.

Elías, Eduardo. "Sandra Cisneros." *Dictionary of Literary Biographies*. Karen Rood, ed. Vol. 122. Detroit: Gale Research Inc., 1992, 77–81.

Elliott, Gayle. "An Interview with Sandra Cisneros." *The Missouri Review* 25, no. 1 (2002): 96–109.

Estill, Adriana. "Building the Chicana Body in Sandra Cisneros' *My Wicked Wicked-Ways*." *Rocky Mountain Review of Language and Literature* 56, no. 2 (2002): 25–43.

Estrada Shuru, Xochitl. *The Poetics of Hysteria in Chicana Writing: Sandra Cisneros, Margarita Cota-Cárdenas, Pat Mora, and Bernice Zamora*. PhD diss. Albuquerque: Univ. of New Mexico Press, 2000.

Eysturoy, Annie. *Daughters of Self-Creation: The Contemporary Chicana Novel.* Albuquerque: Univ. of New Mexico Press, 1996.

Ganz, Robin. "Border Crossings and Beyond." *MELUS* 19, no. 1 (1994): 19–29.

García, Ignacio M. *Chicanismo: The Forging of a Militant Ethos Among Mexican Americans.* Tucson: Univ. of Arizona Press, 1997.

Gaspar de Alba, Alicia. "Literary Wetback." *Infinite Divisions: An Anthology of Chicana Literature,* Tey Diana Rebolledo and Eliana S. Rivero, eds. Tucson: Univ. of Arizona Press, 1993, 288–292.

González, Rodolfo. *I Am Joaquín/Yo Soy Joaquín: An Epic Poem.* New York: Bantam, 1972; previously self-published in 1967.

González-Berry, Erlinda. Review of *Woman Hollering Creek and Other Stories* by Sandra Cisneros, *The Americas Review* 20, no.1 (Spring 1991): 83–85.

Graff, Kier. "Caramel." *Audio for Adults* (March 1, 2003): 1213.

Gutérrez y Muhs, Gabriella. "Sandra Cisneros and Her Trade of the Free Word." *Rocky Mountain Review* (Fall 2006): 23–36.

Hernández Cruz, Victor. "Mountains in the North: Hispanic Writing in the U.S.A." *Americas Review* 14, no. 3–4 (Fall–Winter, 1986): 110–114.

Hoffert, Barbara. "Cisneros, Sandra, *Loose Woman:* Poems." *Library Journal* (May 15, 1994): 76.

Horno-Delgado, Asunción, et al., eds. *Breaking Boundaries: Latina Writing and Critical Readings.* Amherst, MA: Univ. of Massachusetts Press, 1989.

Johnson González, Bill. "The Politics of Translation in Sandra Cisneros's *Caramelo.*" *Differences: A Journal of Feminist Cultural Studies* 17, no. 3 (2006): 3–19.

Jussawalla, Ferroza, and Reed Way Dasenbrock, eds. *Interviews with Writers of the Post-colonial World.* Jackson: Univ. of Mississippi Press, 1992. 2287–2306.

Kingston, Maxine Hong. *The Woman Warrior.* New York: Vintage, 1989.

Lanser, Susan Snaider. *Fictions of Authority: Women Writers and Narrative Voice* Ithaca: Cornell Univ. Press, 1992.

Lowry, Kathy. "The Purple Passion of Sandra Cisneros." *Texas Monthly* 25, no. 10 (October 1997): 148–150.

Luis, William. *Dance Between Two Cultures: Latino Caribbean Literature Written in the United States.* Nashville: Vanderbilt Univ. Press, 1997.

Marin, Marguerite V. *Social Protest in an Urban Barrio: A Study of the Chicano Movement.* Lanham, MD: Univ. Press of America, 1991.

McCracken, Ellen. "Sandra Cisneros (1954–)." *Latino and Latina Writers.* Alan West-Duran, et al., eds. New York: Thomson/Gale, 2004: 229–249.

Mesic, Penelope. "Sandra Cisneros." *Contemporary Literary Criticism* 69, Detroit: Gale Research, 1992, 144.

Mirriam-Goldberg, Caryn. *Sandra Cisneros: Latina Writer and Activist.* Berkeley Heights, NJ: Enslow Publishers, 1998.

Morales, Ed. "Imaginary Homeland, Interview: Sandra Cisneros." *Críticas* (September/October 2002): 29–32.

Mullen, Harryette. "A Silence Between Us Like a Language: The Untranslatability of Experience in Sandra Cisneros's *Woman Hollering Creek.*" *MELUS* 21, no. 2 (Summer 1996): 3–20.

Niño, Raúl. "The Booklist Interview, Sandra Cisneros." *Booklist* (September 1, 1993): 36–37.

Novas, Himilce. *Everything You Need to Know About Latino History.* New York: Plume, 2003.

Olivares, Julian. "Entering *The House on Mango Street.*" *Teaching American Ethnic Literatures,* John R. Maitano and David R. Peck, eds. Albuquerque: Univ. of New Mexico Press, 1996, 2209–2235.

Prida, Dolores. "*Beautiful Señoritas.*" *Hispanic American Literature,* Nicolás Kanellos, ed. New York: Longman, 1995, 293–322.

Queirós, Carlos. "Facing Backwards," http://www.aarpsegundajuventud.org/english/entertainment/2009-SPR/sandra_cisneros_qa.html (Accessed April 3, 2009).

Quintana, Alvina. "Borders Be Damned: Creolizing Literary Relations." *Cultural Studies* 13, no. 2 (1999): 358–368.

Rebolledo, Tey Diana. *Women Singing in the Snow: A Cultural Analysis of Chicana Literature.* Tucson: Univ. of Arizona Press, 1995.

Rendón, Armando. *The Chicano Manifesto.* Berkeley, CA: Ollin and Associates, 1996; originally published in 1971.

Rimer, Sara. "Novelist's Purple Palette Is Not to Everyone's Taste." *New York Times* (July 13, 1998), http://www.nytimes.com/ref/membercenter/nytarchive.html (Accessed May 12, 2008).

Rodriguez Aranda, Pilar E. "On the Solitary Fate of Being Mexican, Female, Wicked, and Thirty-three: An Interview with Sandra Cisneros." *The Americas Review* 19, no.1 (1990): 64–80.

Romero, Mary, Pierrette Hondagneu-Sotelo, and Vilma Ortiz, eds. *Challenging Frontera: Structuring U.S. Latina and Latino Lives.* New York: Routledge, 1997.

Rosales, Francisco A. *Chicano! The History of the Mexican American Civil Rights Movement.* Houston: Arte Público Press, 1996.

Rubenstein, Roberta. *Boundaries of the Self: Gender, Culture, Fiction.* Urbana: Univ. of Illinois Press, 1987.

Saeta, Elsa. "An Interview with Ana Castillo." *MELUS* 22, no. 3 (1997):133–149.

Sagel, Jim. "Sandra Cisneros." *Publishers Weekly* (March 29, 1991): 74–75.

Sánchez, Ricardo. *Hechizospells.* Los Angeles: Univ. of California/LA Chicano Studies Series, 1976.

Sanders, Scout Russell. "The Most Human Art: Ten Reasons Why We'll Always Need a Good Story." *Georgia Review.* (September–October 1997): 54–56.

Satz, Marta. "Returning to One's House: An Interview with Sandra Cisneros." *Southwest Review* 82, no. 2 (Spring 1997): 166–185.

Schultheis, Arianne. "Sandra Cisneros Plays with the Notion of Boundaries." *New University Online.* http://www.newuniversity.org/plain_article.php?id=1629 (Accessed February 19, 2008).

Sedano, Michael. "*House on Mango Street:* A Novel Hits the Hustings." http://www.labloga.blogaspot.com/2005/03/house-on-mango-street-novel-hits.html (Accessed November 1, 2007).

Soto, Gary. "Sandra Cisneros," *Contemporary Literary Criticism.* Vol. 69. Detroit: Gale Research, 1992, 144–145.

Spender, Dale. *The Writing or the Sex?* New York: Pergamon, 1989.

Stavans, Ilan. "Familia Facres: *Caramelo.*" *Nation* 276, no. 5 (February 10, 2003), http://www.thenation.com/docprem.mhtml?!=20030210&s=stavans (Accessed February 19, 2008).

Stefanko, Jacqueline. "New Ways of Telling: Latinas' Narratives of Exile and Return." *Frontiers: A Journal of Women's Studies* 17, no. 2 (1996): 50–69.

Steiner, Stan. *La Raza: The Mexican Americans.* New York: Harper Collins, 1986.

Suárez, Ray. "Conversation: Cisneros." *Online NewsHour,* http://www.pbs.org/newhour/conversation/july-dec02/cisneros_10-15.html (Accessed February 19, 2008).

Tabor, Mary B. W. "A Solo Traveler in Two Worlds." *New York Times* (January 7, 1993): C1, C10.

Thomson, Jeff. "'What Is Called Heaven': Identity in Sandra Cisneros's Woman Hollering Creek." *Studies in Short Fiction* 33, no. 3 (Summer 1994): 415–424.

Torres, Héctor. "Story, Telling, Voice: Narrative Authority in Ana Castillo's *The Mixquiahuala Letters.*" *Chicana (w)rites: On Word and Film.* Ann Arbor: Univ. of Michigan Press, 1994, 143.

———. "Sandra Cisneros: Two Interviews." *Conversations with Contemporary Chicana and Chicano Writers.* Albuquerque: Univ. of New Mexico Press, 2007: 191–243.

TuSmith, Bonnie. *All My Relatives: Community in Contemporary Ethnic American Literature.* Ann Arbor: Univ. of Michigan Press, 1994.

Trujillo, Carla. *Chicana Lesbians: The Girls Our Mothers Warned Us About.* San Francisco: Aunt Lute Press, 1990.

Valdéz, Luis. *Early Works: Actos, Bernabe, and Pensamiento Serpentino.* Houston: Arte Público Press, 1990.

Vigil, Evangelina. *Woman of Her Word: Hispanic Women Write.* Houston: Arte Público Press, 1987.

Villarreal, José Antonio. *Pocho.* New York: Anchor Books, 1970; first published in 1959; Spanish translation by Doubleday, 1994.

Wyatt, Jean. "On Not Being La Malinche: Border Negotiations of Gender in the Works of Sandra Cisneros." *Studies in Women's Literature* 14, no. 2 (April 1995): 243–271.

Index

About the Author

CARMEN HAYDÉE RIVERA received her B.A. and M.A. in British and American Literature from the University of Puerto Rico and holds a Ph.D. in Multiethnic Literatures of the U.S. from Northeastern University. She has taught courses in American Literature, Puerto Rican Writers in the United States, and Contemporary U.S. Latino/a Literature. She was the co-editor of a collection of essays titled *Writing off the Hyphen: New Perspectives on the Literature of the Puerto Rican Diaspora*, and her work has appeared in such journals as *The Ethnic Studies Review, Centro Journal*, and *Sargasso*.

DATE DUE

1994	APR 1 7 1997
FEB 2 5 1993	APR 1 5 1997
RETURNED	
MAY 0 3 1993	MAR 1 1999
MAY 0 7 1993	
RETURNED	JAN 0 4 1999
MAR 0 1	RETURNED
	APR 2 7 1999
FEB 1 7 1994	
RETURNED	DEC 2 3 1999
APR 1 9 1994	
APR 0 7 1994	DEC 1 5 1999
RETURNED	
OCT 2 4 1994	
RETURNED	
NOV 2 8 1995	
NOV 2 0 1995	
RETURNED	
JAN 1 1 1997	
FEB 0 6 1996	